D0843725

Blakely
ISLAND IN TIME

by

JoAnn Roe

MONTEVISTA PRESS
Bellingham, Washington

OTHER BOOKS BY JoANN ROE:
The North Cascadians (Madrona Publishers, Seattle)
The Real Old West (Douglas & McIntyre, Vancouver B.C.)
Frank Matsura, Frontier Photographer (Madrona Publishers, Seattle)
F.S. Matsura (Heibonsha Publishers, Tokyo)
The Columbia River (Fulcrum Publishers, Golden CO)
Seattle Uncovered (Seaside Press, imprint of Wordware, Houston)
The North Cascades Highway
        (Mountaineers Books, Seattle, reprinted by Montevista Press, Bellingham)
Stevens Pass
        (Mountaineers Books, Seattle, reprinted by Caxton Press, Caldwell ID)
Ranald MacDonald, Pacific Rim Adventurer
        (Washington State University Press, Pullman WA)
Ghost Camps & Boom Towns (Montevista Press, Belllingham)
Children's books: *Castaway Cat, Fisherman Cat, Alaska Cat*, and
        Samurai Cat (Montevista Press, Bellingham)

Blakely Island In Time

Dedicated to the Children and Grandchildren

Of Ernest and JoAnn Burkhart

Who have grown up on Blakely Island

ACKNOWLEDGMENTS:

My gratitude and profound thanks to the dozens of Blakely Island people who have shared their memories and anecdotes with me. Outside sources of information are listed in the bibliography at the end of this book. In addition, I thank my editors who pored through the materials and pointed out changes that needed to be made, and those who shared their photographs for use in the book. I appreciate the attention to complex details in the preparation of the book for publication by John Madden, Jr., and the staff of AAA Printing Company.

Inevitably, past events are remembered differently by participants. The author trusts that any differences in and omissions of memoirs simply will become topics of lively conversations in the future.

CONTENTS

Chapter I
BEGINNINGS

The story of Blakely Island begins in the misty past. About 600 million years ago today's San Juan Islands, including Blakely Island, did not exist. In essence, they drifted in from who knows where later in geologic time. The western edge of North America was somewhere near today's Idaho-Washington border in the pre-Cambrian era. During the following Paleozoic time period, 570 to 245 million years ago, the western coasts did not exist, either. Gradually shallows spread westward from the "beach" and, little by little, rocks and pieces of land found their way to create the Pacific Northwest as we know it.

Uplifts created the North Cascades Mountains. Gradually the resultant lake between them and the Rocky Mountains dried up. Lands west of the Cascades emerged and islands offshore. Movement of rocks is described as a horizontal sheet of material moving west or northwest from the North Cascades Mountains over materials of an earlier time. Underlying our San Juan Islands most material was from the Shuksan Thrust Fault moving in horizontal slices from south of Mount Baker through the Skagit Valley toward the San Juans and Vancouver Island in Mesozoic or Paleozoic times. Later bits and pieces of the earth docked along the continental shelves from elsewhere, overlying the prior materials from the Shuksan Thrust. Indeed, rocks of the San Juan Islands are so similar to those of northern California that they may have come from there.

Geologists David Alt and Donald Hyndman wrote that our islands include igneous rocks: pillow basalts, gabbro, and quartz diorite. Andesites occur deriving from the North Cascades volcanoes. Sedimentary rocks like muddy sandstone and small amounts of chert and limestone came from the shallow seas mentioned above that eventually were covered up by other rocks. Bates McKee, geologist and author of the book *Cascadia*, assigns Blakely Island as containing Jurassic-Cretaceous sedimentary rocks and volcanic rocks of the Nooksack, Deer Point, and Spieden types. The oldest rocks in the islands are gneisses and granites.

Making a giant step forward again: On one typical day the morning dawned bright and sunny on a steamy jungle of forested mountains that jutted from the tropical foliage. Dinosaurs browsed on the lush greenery. Sea creatures multiplied in the waters around Blakely. Miles to the north in today's Alaska animals grazed in this same warm jungle. In a fateful moment one non-typical day an unknown cataclysm occurred. Some speculate that a large asteroid struck the earth so hard that the poles changed about 90 degrees. Instead of north and south orientation that had created a west coast jungle, the equator changed to its present east-west direction. Far to the north evidence of chaotic conditions surrounded this upheaval. In the 1900s an animal was excavated from an instant freeze, greenery still in its mouth.

Perhaps then, perhaps later, the earth became very cold far south from the new pole. Successive flows of ice overwhelmed everything and everybody (if there were bodies then). Inexorably the ice forged southward, completely covering today's Orcas, San Juan, Lopez, Blakely, and other San Juan islands to a depth of around 5,000 feet. The moving wall of ice shoved boulders and debris ahead to a point beyond Renton and Olympia. Seattle would have been buried under 3412 feet of glacial ice. Nothing lived. What drainage there was reached the sea through the Chehalis River. The glacier overwhelmed the forests of the North Cascades foothills, etching its limits on the mountain rocks, visible yet today, most clearly seen on the bare sides of Church Mountain northwest of Mount Baker.

Time passed and the earth warmed. At least four times the glaciers came and went. At last about 13,000 years ago, the Canadian glaciers melted and did not return, exposing Blakely Island. Like the other islands it was a mountain top surrounded by lakes and troughs. The unimaginable volume of water from melting ice filled the lakes between the islands and rose to great heights as much as 120 feet above the present

Sound levels. It created so much water that sea and fresh water merged through the Strait of Juan de Fuca. As great as it was, the volume of water was nothing when absorbed by the vast Pacific Ocean, and the salt water poured into the former lake beds to envelop the exposed mountain tops and make them islands in the sea. At least four deep basins constitute the Sound's bed. The average depth of the Sound is 450 feet, and the deepest hole about 970 feet is just north of Seattle along Admiralty Inlet.

When things finally settled down, Blakely's geologic heritage did not change much thereafter except that, during the 1962 Alaskan earthquake, the seabed on the northwest shore of Blakely rose a few inches and stranded a sailboat in the Blakely Marina until the entrance was dredged. The bulk of Blakely Island retained its ancient rock of the Jurassic Period except for the northwest section where most homes are located, which is continental drift or miscellaneous materials from the advancing and retreating glaciers during the Pleistocene Era, much more recent in geologic time. The island is just under 5,000 acres or around four miles long and three miles wide.

Taking another huge leap forward in geologic time, the rise and fall of fresh and salt water left clues about creatures such as fossils of tropical leaves and shells on the exposed cliffs along Chuckanut Bay south of Bellingham and at places in the San Juans. For thousands of years the lovely islands of the San Juan group lay silently in what came to be known as Puget Sound, gradually acquiring conifer forests, madrona or arbutus trees, grasses and animals-deer, raccoons, squirrels. Birds proliferated, especially the eagles, ravens, herons, osprey, and seagulls.

Europeans came. First known was Juan de Fuca, a Greek sailing under the flag of Spain in 1592. Whether he sailed among the islands is unknown. The islands slept in the sun and occasional northeast storms for another two hundred years, enjoyed part-time by the native Americans from the mainland. Next came Spaniard Francisco Eliza in 1791, who sent his First Pilot Juan Pantoja y Arriago in the small ship *Santa Saturnina* from Esquimalt (Victoria) to explore. He headed northward on Haro Strait into the Gulf Islands and, bedeviled by strong winds, was forced southward toward Rosario Strait. Along the way he noted the ducks on an island he named Patos and possibly Matia. One wonders at the origin of this name, because the Spanish word is a past tense of "kill, slaughter, etc." Pantoja turned back to Esquimalt because of weather. No mention was made of his wending his way through the islands, so probably he did not go to Victoria past Blakely.

The Spanish expedition moved its base to Port Discovery south of Port Townsend and sent Don Jose Maria Narvaez to explore the southern islands. Quite likely, he skirted the southerly ends of Lopez and San Juan but neither he nor Pantoja mentioned going into the archipelago of San Juan Islands. Temporarily the Spanish suspended their explorations until 1792, sending two new 47-foot brigantines to Esquimalt after last minute outfitting at Nootka Sound on the outside of Vancouver Island. These were the *Sutil* commanded by Dionisio Alcala-Galiano and the *Mexicana* under Cayetano Valdes.

On June 10, they sailed from Victoria south of San Juan and Lopez islands and turned north into Rosario Strait and on northeast past Anacortes, into Bellingham Bay, Hale's Passage and along the mainland shores now known as Sandy Point. Alarmed by the sight of other foreign ships at anchor at Birch Bay on the mainland near today's Blaine (Vancouver's ships), they sped northward toward the Gulf Islands. Unknown to them until the sighting, Captain George Vancouver's vessels were exploring the area at this same time. The Spaniards named several islands as they went: Lopez (a man), San Juan (St. John), Orcas (whales), Guemes (a Spaniard), Fidalgo (Salvador Fidalgo, Spanish explorer and cartographer), Sucia ("dirty" from a nautical viewpoint, i.e., many rocks just under the surface), and Patos and Matia mentioned above. The Spaniards would have missed coasting along Blakely Island.

Meanwhile, on May 18, 1792, Captain George Vancouver and his men in the *Discovery* and the smaller *Chatham* had sailed into the Strait of Juan de Fuca and landed on Protection Island (near Port Townsend) to reconnoiter. Vancouver assigned Lt. William Broughton in the *Chatham* to explore the San Juan Islands. His course took him into the San Juan Channel between Lopez and San Juan Island. He explored both that channel and the Upright Channel between Shaw and Lopez. Fearing rocks and shallows Broughton ordered his small cutter out to tow the brig *Chatham* for awhile. He headed east through Wasp Passage and passed Obstruction Island into Rosario Strait. Thus, Broughton probably was the first European to view the lands of our present settlement and airport.

4

After entering Rosario, Broughton and his small boat had various adventures exploring around Sinclair, Lummi, and Cypress-including avoiding a crash into the rocks at the southeast side of Orcas, borne there by fast tidal action to lose 120 feet of line and lead. They left eventually to summon the larger *Discovery* to join them at Strawberry Bay on Cypress but, upon their return, tide and currents swept the *Chatham* into the reef at the south end of the island. They managed to anchor but were unable to retrieve it later, and it is still down there somewhere. The English adventurers named many of the other islands and Mount Baker on the mainland as they explored, but not Blakely. During his 1841 expedition American Charles Wilkes named our island after Johnston Blakely, a naval officer of the United States, who had been awarded a congressional gold medal for capturing and burning the British brig *Reindeer* during the War of 1812..

As far as can be determined, most of the San Juan Islands were not occupied as permanent home sites by Indian people (I will refer to the Native Americans as Indians because I have been told by modern Indians that this is how they usually refer to themselves), because the Puget Sound groups were regularly harassed by the warlike Southeast Alaskan clans, chiefly the Haidas from the Queen Charlotte Islands or Stikines from the mainland coast. These well-organized and militant people would swoop down in their 11-man war canoes to attack the Puget Sounders, taking their property, killing all they could locate, and kidnapping younger Indians or women to serve as slaves thereafter. They were only one of the coastal peoples to practice slavery and were as brutal in their practices as later English and American settlers were during the slavery period. Even after the Europeans or whites began to settle along Puget Sound shores, the northern raiders came. Early settlers dared not leave their women alone in the house. Isaac Ebey, the Collector of Customs for the Puget Sound District at Port Townsend, was particularly disliked by the northerners. On a dark night, August 11, 1857. northern Indians in war canoes, headed for trouble in Puget Sound, appeared at Ebey's Whidbey Island home, robbed him and beheaded him. As was the custom among some tribes, the marauders took Ebey's head, scalped it, and showed it in several places. After that, they buried the head at Smith Island. Later it was retrieved and buried with Ebey's body.

As late as the early 1900s the battles went on. In a well-recorded incident the northern Indians came down to seek slaves and booty in 1901 and found a large group of Lummi Indians camped out on Eliza Island. Mostly they were women, children, and older people; the men were off hunting in the North Cascades. Falling upon the campers by night the northerners killed most and kidnapped the rest to take back to the Yakutat area as slaves. Tiring of the frequent marauding parties and incensed by the great loss on Eliza Island, the Lummis laid a trap for the northerners during the summer of 1903. Warriors located a good spot a short way up in the Nooksack River and bided their time "at the ready" while scouts checked the Strait of Georgia day and night. Finally, the enemy approached. The Lummis sent out a youth in a fast canoe as bait, making sure that he could be seen. The northern Indians revved up their paddling and pursued the boy right into the Nooksack River, where the Lummi warriors were waiting in ambush and killed all the invaders, said to be hundreds in a book, *Fourth Corner*, by Lelah Jackson Edson, but probably more like dozens.

While the Chinook Indians of the coast ventured toward the San Juans as far as Port Townsend and today's Victoria, and Clallams from the Olympic Peninsula occasionally landed on San Juan, records indicate that the Samish and Lummi tribes were the main people venturing into the San Juan Islands for fishing, hunting, and gathering of plants. Indians called Blakely Island *Hum-Hum-Ilch* for the smell of the tule reeds which grow on the island, much prized for making baskets. Mainland Indians often removed the planks from their longhouses and took them along to provide makeshift shelters at fishing campsites on the islands. The only known campsites on Blakely were the remains of two kitchen middens, rings of stone six feet or more in diameter where the women threw the shells from cooking. One site was on "Signal Point," a sand spit off the south end of the airstrip, lot A. Children playing at that site in the 1960s found arrowheads and such before construction. The other site is hidden under the sand off the north end of the airstrip somewhere. Since Blakely Islanders are familiar with the locations for good clamming and oyster picking, it is logical to assume the Indians were as well aware of the best sites for gathering them. It appears that no permanent ancient native village ever existed on Blakely Island. However, a member of the Coffelt family of Orcas remembers that the Indians had potlatches and gatherings along

Obstruction Pass, possibly where the kitchen middens once existed. Another source asserts that Southeast Alaskan Indians stopped at Thatcher Bay for camas bulbs and tule reeds en route south into Puget Sound to trade and occasionally to plunder or fight with local tribes.

In addition to the Native American population, England reigned the Northwest in the 1600s to 1800s, beginning with the establishment of the far-flung empire of the private fur marketing firm, Hudson's Bay Company (HBC). Although no special records exist, undoubtedly fur trappers stopped to light a beach fire and haul in fish for dinner or walked inland to see if fur-bearing animals existed on the islands. HBC established a foothold around today's Roche Harbor on the north end of San Juan Island in 1845, placing hundreds of sheep on the island to fatten and be sold. Pioneer settlers on Orcas believe that HBC also had sheep on Orcas around the Turtleback Range, because their fathers remember the Turtlebacks as being almost bare of trees in the mid-1800s.

I gleaned a bit of information during research on a fascinating mystery, still unsolved, about the replica of a large-sized anchor outlined with rocks that is atop the Turtlebacks. Since the site is on private lands, in the 1970s I had to gain the cooperation of the owner to access it, an arduous trip by 4WD vehicle through overgrown forest trails. Since pioneers told me that the rocks had been there as long as their parents remembered, which was well back in the mid-1800s, I pursued intensive library research thereafter, amplifying the scanty information by interviews with old settlers about the creators of the anchor, and used the material for a published article.

Some speculated that an anchor fluke pointed to tiny Flat Top Island, on which pirates were said to have buried treasure. That old idea caused many to dig around on the island without success. Pioneers said that soldiers from the English and Americans encampments that resulted from San Juan Island's Pig War would picnic on the Turtlebacks. Perhaps they laid out an anchor just for fun. Still other rumors consisted of the unsubstantiated idea, a New Age sort of theory, that a similar style arrow was somewhere on top of a Blakely mountain and a triangle on San Juan. This kept my two sons tramping the wilds of Blakely for an entire summer without results. I consulted with a maritime expert in Seattle about the design of the anchor, which could provide a date. He said the style was one used around 1800 or before but commented that anchor styles change little, and that the persons who laid out the anchor would have laid the rocks somewhat randomly. Furthermore, about 1955 a misguided writer for a Seattle newspaper climbed to the site, sprayed the rocks with white paint so they could better be seen, then flew over the site and took photos. The paint compromised the rocks as historical artifacts, of course. The mystery makes a great island legend, though.

Until the establishment of the international boundary in 1872 between England (Canada was not yet a separate country) and the United States, white settlers began to squat without official claims on the San Juan Island grasslands. At Roche Harbor a lime operation began. Many men had come to the Northwest to search for gold, particularly the rush to the canyons of the Fraser River and to Barkerville, farther north. A few returned to permanently settle in the islands. After the international border was established along Haro Strait, not Rosario, giving most of the San Juan Islands to the United States, adventurous men or families began to populate the islands, but Blakely slept serenely for awhile.

*William Harrison Coffelt, pioneer
Thatcher Bay Mill owner.*

Paul K. Hubbs

E.C. Gillette

The original Horseshoe Lake Cabin built by Harrison Coffelt.
Courtesy of Robert J. and Joan W. Coffelt.

Horseshoe Lake Cabin. The addition built by Menzies is at right.

Chapter II
PIONEER TIMES

Blakely Island's seven or eight square miles of mountain top were heavily covered with conifers, mostly Douglas fir and hemlock. Two natural lakes, Spencer and Horseshoe, the latter especially deep, provided plentiful water. Each is about 70 acres in size. Until modern methods of checking depth were used, no one knew how deep are some holes in the center of the lake. According to oral history or legend an unknown person in the mid-1900s checked the depth of Horseshoe and ran out of cord at 375 feet. A persistent legend is that then dye dumped into Horseshoe Lake came up in Lake Crescent on the Olympic Peninsula. Were that true, there would have to be an ancient lava tube between the two that passes very deeply under Puget Sound. It makes an interesting theory, at least. A 1975 bulletin by the Washington Department of Ecology by John T. Whetter, "Geology and Water Resources of the San Juan Islands," debunks the theory, stating there are no underground streams beneath the islands. Dr. Ross Shaw of Seattle Pacific University (SPU) Blakely campus and a student did a personal survey in 1981, thereafter declaring that Horseshoe Lake was carved out of bedrock by glaciers, and that the lake is 95 feet deep in the center, has an average depth of 47 feet. and its watershed is one square mile. OK, but couldn't the bedrock have a leak in it??? I like that theory better; it's much more romantic.

The beautiful green island was not settled until the mid-1800s. Blakely Island's officially acknowledged first white resident was Paul K. Hubbs, Jr., who moved from San Juan Island with his wife Sasha to homestead. Before that Hubbs, son of a well-born Tennessee lawyer, was Deputy Collector of Customs on San Juan Island.

Hubbs' introduction to the San Juan Islands was not the most peaceful. He had been a scout during the 1856 Indian wars of eastern Washington, serving under Major J. Van Bokkelen, who subsequently was appointed Customs Collector at Port Townsend. On April 20, 1857, he appointed Hubbs as a Deputy to serve on San Juan Island, a venue still not legally acknowledged as even belonging to the United States. Just one year later the Clallam Indians came to the island by night and fired into Hubbs' cabin but failed to hit their target. They retreated to their camp after neighbor Charles Griffin, the manager of the sheep farm owned by the Hudson's Bay Company known as Bellevue Farm, heard the shots and went to Hubbs' assistance. Griffin then contacted Port Townsend authorities, who sent soldiers by boat to deal with the matter. The Clallams quickly fled back to their Olympics.

Hubbs was really the only American presence or authority on the San Juan Island for a time. He had to deal with rescuing gold miners who were attacked by Indians on various island shores. Despite disputed ownership of the islands, he tried to collect customs fees from settlers. To his lot fell the political problems inherent in the dual claims of ownership by the English and Americans.

While Kaiser Wilhelm was weighing the matter of whether the international boundary should go through Haro Strait or Rosario Strait, the simmering tensions between England and the Americans flared from an unlikely and simple incident. The Englishman owned an errant pig that invaded the American's garden, aggravating him until he shot the pig in 1859. An international uproar resulted. As is well covered in books about San Juan Island's "Pig War," matters escalated until the English settled troops at the north end near Roche Harbor and the Americans a similar encampment at the south end. It was easy duty for both camps, which tended to compete in athletic events and meet for dinners instead of waging war. Would that subsequent wars would have been conducted this way!

Hubbs and others negotiated with the English and dealt with American military figures such as General William Harney and the Northwest's own Captain George Pickett then stationed at Bellingham. The boundary dispute was settled, and not long after Paul Hubbs and his wife sought the solitude of Blakely Island. He appears to have secured sole ownership of the entire island, since he is on San Juan

County census records in 1870 as having been granted the exclusive privilege to an island about five square miles. He ran 400 sheep on the island, but on the 1880 records for Blakely he had no wife and was listed as a fisherman. His sole ownership may have been an assumption because soon other settlers are listed as owners.

Although Hubbs is officially listed as the first property owner of Blakely, from recent research it appears that Hubbs was not the first white family to live there. The Reed family of Decatur Island was the first white resident family to live on Blakely, perhaps temporarily and, no doubt, as non-owners. Decatur Island officially claims her, but Isabelle Reed, daughter of John and Mary (Tacee) Reed, was the first known child born on Blakely. She came into the world at the south end of Blakely Island on March 16, 1867, according to her published obituary. Because her parents dwelled most of the time on Decatur Island, her birth certificate shows her birthplace as Decatur. The Reeds had rafted some oxen from Fairhaven (Bellingham) to Blakely Island for logging purposes and lived there for some time, during which Isabelle was born. Because of insufficient grazing land for the oxen the Reeds moved over to Decatur a bit later. When she became an adult, Isabelle married John T. Jones, a Welsh immigrant and spent most of her life on Decatur. Jones' cousin, Thomas T. Jones, lived on Blakely for several years, and ran sheep on Blakely, Obstruction, and Frost islands around 1890 to 1900.

Hubbs activities on Blakely are little known. Old records seem to show that he sold the *island* to Edward. C. Gillette, but Gillette is listed as going to Blakely in 1874 to raise sheep on the southeast side and not the entire island According to David Richardson, author of the fine book, *Pig War Islands*, Hubbs thereafter decided to live with the Indians instead of the whites and moved away. (Could it be that the shenanigans that he had lived through on San Juan Island influenced him?) Gillette had worked closely with Hubbs on San Juan. As mentioned earlier, Hubbs was a Deputy Customs man and Gillette its first surveyor, arriving in February 1858 to assist a group of Americans seeking to file land claims. He eventually became San Juan County's superintendent of schools.

Gillette was credited with helping Captain Pickett confront and suppress the rampant disregard for the law on the island in the 1860s. At that time waves of miners heading for Barkerville and the Fraser River gold rush diggings came through Puget Sound. In 1858 the hordes of men bushwhacked their way through Whatcom County's tall forests toward today's Sumas and the Fraser River beyond, the shortest way north. England recognized that its merchants were losing supply opportunities to Bellingham and other American settlements, and authorities passed a law that miners must first get a permit in Victoria (seat of government), before going north to prospect. Thereafter, the Olympic Peninsula, Semiahmoo Spit, and the San Juan Islands (an efficient way to approach Vancouver Island by boat) swarmed with transients heading toward Victoria. After obtaining the permit, prospectors took the shortest way to the gold fields--up the Fraser River toward what is now Hope BC. This course took them past Fort Langley, a Hudson's Bay Company supply post. Of course, it is clear that was the purpose of the required permit. Northern Indians still came to the islands, too, as they had for generations, to look for booty and slaves. Gillette as Justice of the Peace and Captain George Pickett of the U.S. Army had their hands full for a few years.

In 1862 Gillette resigned his post to become a partner with Lyman Cutler (the American who shot the English pig) in a lime operation at Roche Harbor that they called San Juan Lime Company. However, only a year later Gillette sold his interest to Augustin Hibbard. In 1874 Gillette acquired a portion, quite possibly southeast of Seattle Pacific University's (SPU) present site, not the whole of Blakely Island as records seem to indicate. He remained there until 1889, when he sold his land to Richard H. Straub, who succeeded John Vierick as the Blakely Island school teacher. Gillette was still on Blakely, therefore, during the advent of Thatcher mill.

The Coffelt and Vierick families, of which many descendants still live on various San Juan islands, came to the area about the same time as the Reeds of Decatur Island. William Harrison Coffelt and his brother James Monroe Coffelt, two sons of widowed Elizabeth Coffelt of Kansas, built their own covered wagon and traveled west on the Oregon Trail in 1869 and 1870 to Tacoma. Monroe decided to go south to Oregon and Harrison, after working at logging camps and other jobs, wound up on Orcas Island and built a cabin for himself at Grindstone Bay.

The San Juans were not too safe in the 1870s. As mentioned earliler, Northern Indians came south to kidnap the mostly Salish Indian (locals) women as spouses. The few white residents of Orcas and Blakely were in danger, as well. Hostilities did not ebb until the latter part of the 19th century. Most of the local and peaceful Indian people who did dare to live on the islands had homes on Orcas or San Juan.

Around 1881 Eastsound consisted only of Shattuck's Store, a post office within the store, a log schoolhouse nearby, and a log building with a lean-to that served as a hotel. Soon a newcomer, Elder Gray, organized a church and helped organize an Orcas Island Canning Company and Orcas Island Buying Company. Residents then found apple orchards and prune trees to be good commercial crops.

Younger brother Jasper and Elizabeth joined Harrison Coffelt in 1873. They arrived on Orcas, passing Blakely Island through Thatcher Pass, on the paddlewheeler *Ancon*, the chief island transportation at the time. It was an ungainly vessel that resembled a long Indian canoe, low to the water with a pointed bow and square stern. It flew both the American flag and the Pacific SS Mail flag blackened by the smoke pouring out of her stack. According to the records of the Coffelt family, while the boat passed Thatcher Bay, Harrison told his mother that he just awaited enough capital to set up a shop there to manufacture steam engines, as well as establish a lumber mill. While he accumulated the funds, Harrison worked intermittently on Blakely while living mostly on Orcas Island. Elizabeth spent one summer with him at his cabin near Thatcher and established a garden near Spencer Lake.

Within a few years of Elizabeth's arrival on Orcas the remaining members of her family (except Monroe) moved to Washington. Coffelts homesteaded land on Lopez Island, where descendants still live at this writing. Meanwhile on Orcas Island the Coffelts had become close friends of John Vierick, a hardy Prussian immigrant who had been a ship captain between Washington and Alaska before settling around Doe Bay. In 1879 his daughter Anna was married to Harrison Coffelt, uniting the two families who were involved in the Thatcher Bay Mill on Blakely.

The Viericks and Coffelts of Doe Bay thought that logging on Blakely would be a money-making windfall and cut a million board feet of timber on the island, only to discover that the logs were of poor quality. The rocks and minimal top soil made the trees grow crooked and gnarly, not so good for lumber. However, near the Horseshoe Lake cabin built by Harrison, the families did cut good stands of cedar for log cabins and shakes.

From the book *Time and Lives of Some Coffelts in America* Harrison is quoted as saying that the hill above the Lower Lake (Spencer) also was heavily forested with old cedars three to five feet in diameter, as well as alder, red fir, yellow pine, Douglas fir, and white fir. For building cabins he said:

> *At each of the ends, the logs were notched first using a scribe to mark the matches, then we axed out the wood and smoothed the notch with a gouge.One log fitted snugly over the other.*

> *The cracks were chined with triangular shaped cedar rails. The cedars had split insides for a flatter interior surface. For surfacing, the log was scored with a score axe and then the chips removed with a broad axe or adz. Care had to be taken to prevent barking the knuckles.*

> *Cedar shakes were used for the roof. The sides were fitted with two windows on one side and three on the other side.*

Instead of just logging the island and building cabins (William) Harrison Coffelt and William H. Vierick, his brother-in-law, decided to establish a mill in the late 1870s to take advantage of the water power created by overflow from Spencer Lake into Thatcher Bay. Vierick had owned the property earlier but entered into an agreement with Coffelt to build the mill. With the assistance of his brother John, Coffelt completed an operational mill by 1879. It utilized a reciprocal saw, not a circular saw, powered by the water flow. The output was sufficient to produce enough lumber to build his house at Thatcher Bay. Al Coffelt, Harrison's son , remembered his father building the mill. In the book, *River Pigs & Cayuses*, Al said:

> *He framed that mill, built all the parts, the timbers, braces, and everything. To hold the braces he'd bore a hole through the timbers and drive in wooden pins.*

There was no iron bolts around. Then they had a mill-raising. I guess everybody from all around the whole country was there. I remember I stood on the hill and looked down to see them. A lot of men hauling with block and tackle putting the mill up. They got it up in a day.

Coffelt and Vierick continued to develop the mill and eventually added steam power (an engine and boiler). Water power was adequate for the reciprocal saw, but steam was better for the new circular saw they added. The mill produced lumber and box "shook," the lumber needed to put together boxes for fruit or fish handling. Harrison's real aim, however, was to have a shop where he could develop machinery for commercial purposes. While he was at Thatcher, he did develop cannery equipment, and later on Lopez Island some credited him with developing the cannery machine called the "Iron Chink," widely used in the Northwest for cutting up salmon   He said in the Coffelt book that he sold it to the Island Packing Company under a verbal agreement involving future rights and also was instrumental in developing a crimping machine for the canning industry.

As another product line Coffelt and his father made seine boats for others out of drift logs, good cedar ones that had escaped from booms. They ran them through the saw mill and planed them to size, used square galvanized nails, and mixed their own paint out of white lead and linseed oil. To avoid paying twenty-five cents for a pair of metal oarlocks, the Coffelts put in pins like the Navy used on its boats. They carved out the oars from cedar, using a draw knife. The price for the boats was about a dollar per foot. When the Thatcher mill stopped making boxes for fruit and fish, the men produced herring boxes and delivered them to a herring fishery on the spit at Waldron Island.

Despite the varied products they manufactured, Al Coffelt remembered that under President Grover Cleveland business was scarce and cash money hard to get, that people worked in logging camps and saw mills for as little as five cents an hour. Like others the Blakely Island people relied on barter, hunting and family gardens. Coffelt recalled that a 50-pound sack of flour was sixty-five cents and 100 pounds of sugar two and a half dollars, and it was all brown sugar. They stored potatoes by digging a pit in the ground. Locals took excess produce to

Bellingham in their home-made boats-double-ender seine boats 24 feet long, six feet beam, propelled by oars. The trip took a whole day unless a wind made sailing possible. Fish and shellfish rounded out the settlers' diets but were worth little as a cash source at the time.

Meanwhile, a scattering of other settlers moved onto Blakely. H.W. Whitener moved from Samish to the northwest end of Blakely in the early 1870s and later was elected sheriff of San Juan County. Until the 1970s or 1980s the remains of a homesteader cabin could be seen north of the summit of "Old Steepie" (a hill on the main road to Horseshoe Lake). Another cabin was across the lake and one near today's pump house. I have been unable to determine who owned them. A barn at Armitage Bay possibly was built by the Reeds or Jones but has vanished. At the time of Gillette's residence on Blakely (until 1889), J.C. and Pauline Burns resided on the adjacent land which extended inland from the southwest side of the island. Burns worked for a railroad and his wife remained at the Blakely home. Gillette sold his land to Richard Straub, making him the neighbor of Burns, an unhappy situation described later.

Despite the ongoing sawmill operation, prospectors came to Blakely around 1900 to do mineral exploration at a site on Bald Bluff and on the eastern shore. The Bald Bluff effort only resulted in about a 10-foot drift or tunnel from the base of the mountain, but along the eastern shore prospectors sank a shaft about 100 feet deep and a drift in from the water to intersect it. Rumor was that the samples assayed at $18 a ton, but no ore ever was shipped. The identity of the prospectors has been lost over time. Although no deep shafts have actually been found, IF they are there, they are extremely dangerous. Curiosity seekers are firmly warned not to access the sites. No one wants to fall into an abandoned shaft

It was Harrison Coffelt who set up the original water system for the Thatcher Mill--a water wheel driven by the stream that steeply descended from Spencer Lake. The water wheel was coupled to reduction gear with a leather belt and glued with cow parts. By 1884 the system used a series of log pipes or open flumes leading from Spencer Lake. The line shaft was supported overhead by intermittent bearings, according to Harrison in the Coffelt book. In 1887 he installed a steam engine powered by a wood-fired boiler. A series of pipes moved a piston which, in turn, rotated a crank shaft and then a fly wheel. The system was similar to that used in boats of the period. It was efficient enough to create limited electricity, as well. It is said that this was the first electricity produced in the San Juan Islands.

In the memoirs contained in the book, *Times and Lives of Some Coffelts in America*, Harrison related how the mill worked:

> We had boom men taking care of the bull pen, guiding the logs to the drag chain. The logs rolled off the conveyor onto the cold deck. The carriage man dogged the logs in place against the bolsters, in order to line up the logs with respect to the circular saw. The carriage moved back and forth to bring the log in contact with the large circular saw. The logs were then squared. The sawer operated the carriage back and forth. The logs were meticulously slabbed into cants. Squared logs were sawed into cants on the head rig. The cants were led through rollers to resaw into lumber.

Between them the two families, Vierick and Coffelt, owned all of Thatcher Bay and the adjacent land up to Spencer Lake. Harrison became the first postmaster at the little store building at the mill site. Catherine Spencer was the first postmistress, followed by Ross Spencer and Shirley Spencer Plummer. In 1888 Coffelt purchased the mill from Vierick.

Intrigued by the readily available water power at Thatcher from the overflow creek that descended from the lake thereafter called Spencer Lake, Theodore Spencer bought the mill and box factory in 1892 and renamed it the Spencer Mill. Spencer had been deputy customs collector from Roche Harbor, scion of a family with descendants today on many of the islands. Spencer felt he could make a go of the mill and did succeed. Harrison continued to operate the mill for Spencer but, after a few years, he resigned and moved to Orcas Island. Nonetheless, as late as 1899, records show that the Coffelts sold logs to the Spencer Mill. Al Coffelt, Harrison's son, returned to Blakely at some time, working at the mill and doing other jobs to make ends meet. Berna Menzies, who lived with her parents at the Horseshoe Lake cabin, remembers attending school in the 1930s with two of Al's sons, Alfred Jr. and Clarence

Ray and Kate Spencer on Lopez Island.

Shirley Plummer, now of Lopez Island, lived most of her youth at Thatcher Bay. She is the daughter of Ray and Kate Spencer. Her husband Buck operated the boat "Blakely".

The original bathtub house or "New Blarney Castle"

The original Thatcher School was built by Harrison Coffelt but was improved and served students until the 1940's.

Thatcher School Interior.

GENERAL PROGRESS REPORT	1st	2nd	3rd	4th	5th	6th	F'l
Scholarship							
Citizenship				/	/	/	/
Effort				2	/	/	/

Qualities Desirable for School Success
Not more than four marks will be given each report

	1st	2nd	3rd	4th	5th	6th	F'l
Courtesy				/			/
Promptness				2	2		
Dependability				2			
Cheerful Cooperation				/	.	/	
Self-reliance				2	/		
Initiative					/	/	
Thrift							
Self-control				2		/	
Good Sportsmanship					2		
School Service				/			/
Good Workmanship							

"1"—Indicates qualities which the pupil possesses or is developing noticeably.
"2"—Indicates qualities less developed, which the pupil should try to strengthen.
"3"—Indicates qualities in which the pupil should make special effort to improve.

IMPORTANT
If the following item is checked, parents should give special thought to improving any condition affecting unfavorably the pupil's work.

Promotion In Danger							

STUDIES—REPORT	1st	2nd	3rd	4th	5th	6th	F
Reading				C	C+	C	
Spelling				B	B	B	
Language				C	C		
Arithmetic				C	C	C+	
Geography				B	A		
History and Civics				B	B		
Agriculture							
Natural Science				A	A	E	
Home Econ's							
Writing				C	C+	C	
Music				A	A		
Drawing and Design				C	B	E	

Health Record							
Hygiene and Health Habits				B	B	C	
Posture							
Weight							

Explanation of Marks
A, B, C, D,—Passable.   X—Not Passable.

Extra School Activities
Participation in the school activities checked deserves recognition.

*Orchestra, Club, etc.

Thatcher Report Card.

Hamilton Family. L to R: Ora, Purley, Durley, Jim or J.E.

Jane Hovde, born Jane Hamilton at Thatcher Bay. Today she is a well-known artist.

The Spencer Mill at Thatcher Bay had the first hydroelectric power in San Juan County to run the mill. The building with the white door at the left was the post office and tiny store. The angled log below the building on the right (which contained the gang saw) was the slip where logs were dragged out of the water. *Courtesy of Buck and Shirley Plummer.*

The Spencer Mill once was the largest north of Seattle.

The Extensive installation at Thatcher Bay.

Spencer Mill has its goods waiting to be loaded onto the boats.

Inside Spencer Mill.

Lumber was loaded onto boats for delivery at Thatcher Bay's pier.

Buck Plummer's Boat "Blakely" was used as a tug for lumbar delivery.

Administration building of the Mill and Post Office at Thatcher Bay.

The post office at Thatcher Bay also carried a small amount of groceries for sale. The building still stood in 1965 but was destroyed by the Spencer Lake washout.

A bridge connected the homes on the cliff to the mill site and sawdust beach.

The Buckeye provided San Juan Islands transportation.

Chapter III
THE SPENCERS

Theodore Spencer moved his family to Blakely and built a home on Spencer Lake at the present site of the Seattle Pacific University facility. When SPU came to the site in 1976, the remains of a cabin-just four walls four or five feet high-were still standing. Across the lake was a logging camp operated by a man named ___Judy. A young couple with school age children lived at the camp, and an old cabin housed transient loggers at the site of the home of BC and Christine Crowley, built in 1981 by Doug Moreton.

Some time before or after 1900, Spencer hired J.E. "Jim" Hamilton and his two sons, Purley and Durley, to improve the hydropower system that ran the mill at Thatcher Bay. The Hamiltons improved and modernized the system fed by water from Spencer Lake rushing at waterfall speed through a deep canyon into Thatcher Bay. Jim Hamilton had experience with hydropower systems as he operated another mill at Anacortes, later ran others on Whidbey Island, and may have had other business interests. Purley and Durley lived on Blakely for several years while they worked at the mill. A third brother Ora drowned while ice skating on one of the lakes.

Eventually, Spencer's numerous brothers and other relatives came to work at the mill, and most of the homes at Thatcher Bay were occupied by a Spencer family member or employee. Two very nice homes on the bluff above the bay have fallen down now, but I remember exploring the deteriorating structures in early 1960. Wallpaper still clung to the walls, and the floors and walls mostly were intact. As late as the 1990s some of the trees near the homes bore fruit. One home was occupied by

Roscoe "Ross" Spencer, Ray's brother. Theodore Spencer's widow Catherine and Jessie, Ray's sister, lived in the other for awhile. Jessie had been a teacher in Portland and lived in the Portland Hotel. She was also the president of the National Teachers Association and had traveled widely. According to Shirley Plummer, she assisted the family financially during hard times. Other homes of workers and family were scattered around Thatcher Bay and have now disappeared entirely or deteriorated.

The Spencer family and its mill remained essentially the only enterprise on Blakely until mid-century. In fact, by 1923 brothers Ray, Roscoe, and relative Dr. Walter Spencer finally acquired the remainder of Blakely Island not already owned by them. Walter and a friend, Dr. Ostrander, both of Portland usually spent a month's vacation on Blakely. Some Coffelts moved to Orcas Island, a few continued at the mill for a time. In its prime years the Spencer Mill was said to be the largest north of Seattle.

Before the turn of the century another rather dashing young man, Robert DeLancy, came from Pennsylvania to work at the mill and lived near Thatcher. Not long afterward he married Lydia, the daughter of John Baldridge of Sedro-Woolley. She bore him two daughters, Clara and Elsie, children who eventually attended the Thatcher School and roamed the island. The girls grew up and left the island. Clara learned the delicate craft of mending rare books, then worked for libraries and schools.

Around 1908 Lydia contracted breast cancer and sought medical help in Bellingham but was pronounced incurable. She returned to Blakely to live out her remaining months, monitored by a hired caregiver. When Clara, who always loved Blakely, returned to the island for a visit, Purley Hamilton was quick to reacquaint himself with her. Romance bloomed and the two were married, uniting the two Blakely families. In 1921 Clara started into labor with their first child almost two months early. The family members carried Clara on a cot down to one of the mill's two tugs, the *Northwest* moored at Thatcher Bay. They discovered that, during a storm the prior night the tug had been banging against the dock and a spike had pierced the hull. It was leaking badly, but the family set out for Anacortes Hospital, anyway. With one man running the bilge pump, the tug continued. Clara's daughter Jane persisted in coming into the world and was born between Cypress and

Blakely Island--right off the black buoy near Cypress. Two months premature she was not expected to live, but she did.

Jane Hamilton lived the first three years of her life at Thatcher Bay and remembers that they called the bluff facing the bay Whale Rock (where several homes were located including the ones mentioned above). She believes that her grandfather DeLancy built the house above the bay, the one still in use. A precocious child she managed to fall into the ocean on her meanderings, and her parents decided to move off the island to more solid land. They joked that she was born on the water and must want to return there. That baby girl today is Jane Hovde of Bellingham, a renowned artist and art instructor. Her works are in major art galleries and collections throughout the West. She and her husband A.J. Hovde, a creative writing professor at Western Washington University, traveled all over the world, living for months at a time in Europe with Jane painting as she went.

Purley Hamilton (as Hamilton Lumber Company, which had mills in Anacortes, Whidbey Island, and Stanwood) purchased a lot next to Blakely marina, where he built a small house for vacations. The house later was used by early caretakers of the island. He bought two additional lots at Driftwood Beach and gave them to Jane and Rose Anne, his daughters. Rose Anne Hamilton became Mrs. Pete Raymond. Jane Hovde no longer has property on Blakely.

Blakely Island was really isolated in the early days with no telephones and boats the only transport for supplies or medical care. Residents seemed to be healthy, though. Even so, Shirley Plummer's brother Jack fell off the dock and broke his arm, not too difficult to fix without a doctor. Another incident was more serious. Catherine Spencer stood too close to the fireplace, her clothing caught fire, and she sustained painful burns. A family member took off by boat to a Lopez phone to summon the Anacortes doctor. The doctor had a fast boat and was at Blakely before the messenger returned. Catherine recovered fully from the freak accident.

A scattering of other residents on Blakely included Bostonian Al Street, who lived in the cabin at today's San Juan Aviation & Yachting Estates (SJAYE) settlement, a cabin later occupied by Doc White. He and his wife raised peas and sold them, and he augmented his income by carpentry. Around 1932 Valeria and Bob Kelton, relatives of Spencers, lived at the north end, probably in the same cabin previously occupied by Street. Kelton worked at the mill sometimes, logged, and did miscellaneous jobs. The couple had four children, among them Mary Ritchie, now of Lopez, the niece of Catherine Spencer (Valeria was Catherine's sister). During the early days of building SJAYE worker Ray Olson lived in a cabin near the south end of the airstrip, a Panabode that had been barged in. Later that cabin and another were combined into the Bob Smythe (52A) cabin. Olson's daughter, Judy Sande of Bellingham, remembers attending school on Orcas Island, transported there by Bartram's boat each day along with the other Blakely children. (More on that later)

Harrison Coffelt built the Horseshoe Lake cabin. His mother Elizabeth and Eliza Coffelt often stayed there in summer, because Elizabeth liked to do gardening on the land nearby that she called Coffelt Flats. Basically the cabin had two rooms-a living room and bedroom, no kitchen. In 1925 or 1926 Alex and Minnie Beatrice "Bun" Menzies moved there with a four-year-old daughter Berna. Alex built on a bedroom for Berna and a kitchen, plus a cooler at the east side of the cabin and a root cellar. Berna recalls that they got water from the lake for most needs and the drinking water from a spring one-fourth mile south. No electricity existed until much later, except at the Spencer Mill. Menzies used kerosene lamps.

Menzies had a white horse named Frank that he used for plowing, any logging required, and transportation; in fact, he built a skid-type sled to haul the Menzies's possessions to Horseshoe Lake. Berna remembers that Frank was very friendly and permitted her and the four Kelton children to ride on its back. She laughed to recall that one would not have room enough, and the horse put its head down so the child could slide off. Berna attended the Thatcher School with many of the Spencer and Coffelt offspring and other millworkers' children. In 1936, when Berna needed to attend high school, the Menzies moved off Blakely.

The next resident of the Horseshoe cabin was a single man, who lived there while working at the mill. Shirley Plummer remembers that he had a heavy beard and the children called him "Haile Selassie," because of his resemblance to the ruler of Ethiopia, but his real name was Henry Patrick. Remains of an old cabin at the south end of the island near Armitage Bay had tattered newspapers still clinging to the walls with the date of 1910. Possibly it was the otherwise unknown resident recalled by Shirley Plummer-a man who built a boat for fishing the waters around Point Lawrence. Shirley also remembers that a house at Homestead Bay also was papered with newspapers.

Most of these early residents worked for the Spencer Mill. The loggers (including the contractor-logger Judy mentioned earlier) used horses to drag logs to Spencer Lake or simply dropped them into the water along the shore. Apparently the loggers also stored logs in the lake near the bathtub house and sent them down into Spencer Lake somehow. On the lake they created a boom from the loose logs and towed it by rowboat with strong oarsmen, later using a small outboard motor, down to the lagoon. This was at the south end of the lake (where today's dirt road over a small dam is located). There they dumped the logs into a log chute that ran down the canyon to the mill at the beach. Vestiges of the old flumes were still visible until 1965, when the dam break washed them away. One year Spencer Lake froze over so solidly that the horses dragged the log booms across the ice! Because the market for logs dried up in the early Depression years, the logging operation ceased in 1929, but the mill continued to operate until 1942 with purchased logs or a backlog that was created from earlier logging..

While Scott McCulloch was a caretaker for SJAYE in the 1970s, he discovered a spring in Spencer Lake while scuba diving. He said, "I had to back away from it, because the water was icy cold. I have no idea where it came from originally, but it was in a spot only about 30 feet deep, yet was as cold as I ever have experienced." Scott is not sure he could find the exact location again, but-from where the lake rafts are moored-it is where the wider part of the lake begins and on the left side. No wonder Spencer is known to have frozen over a few times.

A handful of homesteaders and employees of the mill produced enough children that a school house was necessary. The restored one still standing today was built some time in the 1880s by Harrison Coffelt. It is thought to be the oldest continuously operating school in Washington, as it was in use from 1889 to 1950. In 1889 Richard

Straub, who had purchased E.C. Gillette's holdings, was hired as the teacher. As mentioned earlier, J.C. and Pauline Burns had settled the land next door to Straub. Burns worked on the railroad and was gone much of the time, leaving Pauline to run the small farm and raise their two children. They attended the Thatcher School, where Ray Spencer was a student as early as 1892, along with another dozen or so students.

Pauline had been a Lanterman from Decatur Island, and her brother Leon was a frequent visitor to the Burns home. Straub and the Lantermans were at odds, a feud that came to a tragic head in 1895. The Lantermans and others voiced their suspicions that Straub was looting a small freight steamship J. C. Britain, after it was stranded on Bell Rock and came to question him (why they cared is not known). Straub drove them off with a rifle. Between 1889 and 1895, Pauline was said to have turned the settlers against Straub. Thus, when it came time in 1895 for the school board to approve Straub as the island's school teacher, Burns and Catherine Spencer were two of the three members of the school board and failed to retain Straub. He was particularly incensed at the fact that Leon Lanterman of Decatur, Burns' brother, voted and was not even an islander.

In late August 1895 Leon came to Blakely with Ralph Blythe, his and Pauline's half-brother, to help Pauline with the potato harvest. Irving Parberry, age 17, of a family that homesteaded near Horseshoe Lake, friends of Straub, appeared at the Burns' fence line armed with an axe, and shouted insults at everyone-especially Leon. He accused Leon of setting forest fires on Blakely that had damaged the Parberry's home. Leon walked toward the fence to reason with the boy, whereupon Parberry swung the axe at him. Then Straub leaped up from behind a log with a rifle and fired two shots at Leon, fatally wounding him. Leon called out to his sister Pauline.

Enraged still, Straub shot at Ralph Blythe, who fell to the ground unhurt and played dead. Straub now took after Pauline, yelling that he would kill her next. She ran in a zig-zag pattern toward her home, managing to evade his shots except for sustaining a flesh wound to the shoulder. She got to the house, grabbed her two small boys, and ran to the Spencer home. The Spencers put Pauline and her children into a rowboat and took them to Pauline's parents' home on Decatur.

Meanwhile, Straub returned to put two more bullets into the prone Leon to make sure he was dead before calmly persuading Parberry to get into a boat and go to Friday Harbor. There the pair surrendered voluntarily to the sheriff and were locked up, pending trial.

The funeral of Leon Lanterman attracted substantial numbers of irate islanders, who threatened to storm the Friday Harbor jail and hang Straub. Under cover of darkness the sheriff managed to spirit the two prisoners into the forest and, the next day, get them aboard a U.S. Revenue launch and into a Bellingham jail-narrowly escaping the islanders searching for them. When the trial occurred a month later, Parberry testified for the prosecution and escaped justice, but Straub, Blakely's first teacher, was hanged April 23, 1897, for his crime. He is buried near today's University of Washington Marine Laboratory at Friday Harbor. It was the only recorded hanging in the county of San Juan. Straub may be the only criminal in history who showed the executioner how to tie the noose knot.

After Straub as the teacher of Thatcher School, Blakely's subsequent teachers were a more prosaic lot-mostly interns from Bellingham's Teachers' College (WWU today) who were assigned for either the fall or spring term. Shirley Plummer remembers well attending the old school. Only five or six children attended in the late 1920s. Among the teachers was a Mrs. Marie Carver, who had two girls and boarded with the Ray Spencers that term. Another was a Mrs. Cory with two boys. According to Shirley's memories, one boy, just six years old, hated the family cat and cut off the end of the cat's tail. Another time he put the cat in the oven, but his mother rescued the animal with no harm done. Other teachers were, last names only: Miss Leadbetter, Mrs. Potter, Miss Siler, Mr. Tucker, and Mrs. O'Neil.

Parents of high school age children such as the Menzies, Coffelts and Spencers had to move or to board their children at a city with a high school. Shirley Spencer (Plummer) attended Bellingham High School, staying there with a family. She recalls a wonderful party at her home on Blakely when her family invited the whole class to the island to celebrate the 50th anniversary of Bellingham High.

In 1912 Ray Spencer married Kate (another Katherine) Hitkoe. The young couple homesteaded 160 acres around a small lake about a half-mile cross-country from Spencer Lake adjacent to what locals now call the "bathtub house," a cabin that Ray and Kate Spencer built. Ray believed that his homestead was the last homestead filed in Washington. Because their union produced no children, they adopted a boy and girl orphaned by the death of Kate's sister in 1921 or 1922: the boy Jack, about four, and Shirley Plummer, less than two, now still living on Lopez Island. The couple's first home was, for some odd reason, built in the middle of the marsh just south of the "bathtub house."

In her book of Blakely memories, Plummer wrote:

> Poles had to be laid out to it across the marsh as the marsh filled with water in the winter. ... The house was on very unstable ground. Jack and I used to chase each other around it on the outside and the dishes danced on the inside. All the water was carried from the spring and to use the facilities one dashed across the poles with the water squishing up between them, to the out house.

The Spencers called this house "Old Blarney Castle" and, when Ray built the present bathtub house adjacent to the old log pond, the family called it "New Blarney." The Spencers kept a team of horses, Paul and Queen, for plowing up the garden, logging, and other duties. The family raised bantam chickens, guinea hens, a few cows, and had a black horse named Don and a pony named Major. Ray walked to work at the mill cross country, so careful observers might find traces of his foot trail there yet today. When the family had fulfilled their homestead obligations, they moved to a house right on the sawdust beach adjacent to the mill for a time, then to a fine house on Whale Rock. They moved because the long walk to work caused leg problems for Ray. Like other islanders the couple tended gardens near their home, in the marshy lands just south of Horseshoe Lake, or near Thatcher where some flat ground existed.

Nearby islands were parts of early residents' early lives. Blakely Island was a place of tragedy for the Moore family of Olga on Orcas Island. Joseph and Sarah, who was Chief Seattle's niece, were the town's first homesteaders. Their son Joseph Moore drowned on August 20, 1914, just off Blakely, and his body was never recovered. Later relative Samuel Moore's skiff washed up on Blakely Island and, although the family searched all Blakely's beaches for his body, he also was never found.

Today's Blakely residents accept the flashing light on Obstruction Island as a part of daily life. From 1910 to the l930s it was the duty of the Hodde family on Orcas Island to tend the red light (now green) at the west end of the Obstruction that guided vessels to either Peavine Pass or Obstruction Pass, as well as the white light on the eastern tip. Jane Barfoot Hodde, member of the pioneer family, recalled having picnics on the small beach near the red light across from Blakely.

She remembers well the details of a light tender's job in the islands. All the lights were fueled by kerosene. They had to be adjusted carefully or else the flame would smoke up the chimney so the light would not show clearly, endangering mariners. The lamp itself was similar to the ordinary household kerosene lamp, except the outer glass protection globe was thicker to provide the magnification needed. The round globes were about 10 inches high and eight inches in diameter.

The kerosene container held seven days worth of fuel, requiring a trip once a week to refill the tank and clean the lamps. If a storm was imminent, the light tender would go earlier, especially in winter. Mr. Hodde and, after his death in 1927, his son John walked the three-fourths mile from their home on the east shore of Orcas to the beach to launch a boat to cross Obstruction Pass. The only weather forecasting method the family had was by reading the sky and cloud formations. The Hoddes were familiar with winds and tides, as well as rowing and sailing until the acquisition of a small Evinrude motor modernized their boat trips. As Jane Hodde reported, "The pay for this work wasn't generous, but many times the $13 a month pay was our only cash income."

One of the highlights of her life was the semiannual visit of the lighthouse tender *Heather* which brought kerosene, towels, extra chimneys and other supplies for the lights. The supplies were stored on an 8-foot by 8-foot white-painted storage house near the beach. The kerosene or coal oil came in wooden cases with two five-gallon tins in each. When emptied a tin served many uses around the Hodde farm, such as a repository for water to heat for dishes or baths on the back of the cookstove.

The *Heather* served all the lights in Puget Sound for many years and put on a military face for the benefit of the spectators. Because the water was too deep for the tender to anchor close in, it stopped a long way out from shore. The crew lowered a smaller boat manned by eleven uniformed sailors, who rowed in perfect unison while the coxswain stood in the stern at the tiller. When the boat slowed to beach on shore, the sailors raised their oars vertically then down in smartly maritime unison. In the 1930s the lights were fueled by acetylene gas, eliminating the necessity for regular maintenance and ending the colorful visits of the *Heather*. Today the lights are automated.

Early 1960's aerial view of Blakely grass airstrip and development.

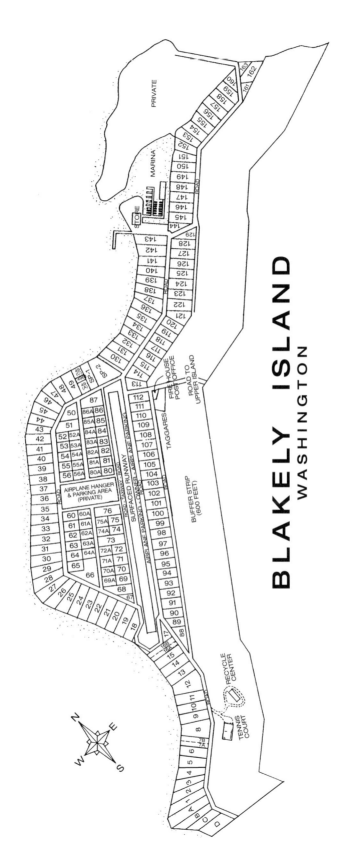

BLAKELY ISLAND

WASHINGTON

42

Early 1960's aerial view of the Blakely Marina.

Believed to be SJAYE before Blakely sirstrip was cleared.

Floyd Johnson showed prospective lot purchasers the lay of the land.

The published list price for lots in the early sixties.

View toward Eastbound in about 1962. Floyd Johnson's panabode in foreground.

Floyd Johnson surveys the San Juan Islands from Blakely Peak.

Betty and Harold Bartram and their Tri-Pacer in 1965. Courtesy of Betty Bartram.

The island Ferry in 1960, beside the Blakely pier. Courtesy of Harold Bartram.

Don & Betty Fitzpatrick's Cabin in 1960's.

Floyd and Ola Johnson enjoy life at their new home near the south end of the airstrip.

Convenient parking next to Dr. Robert Greene's Cabin.

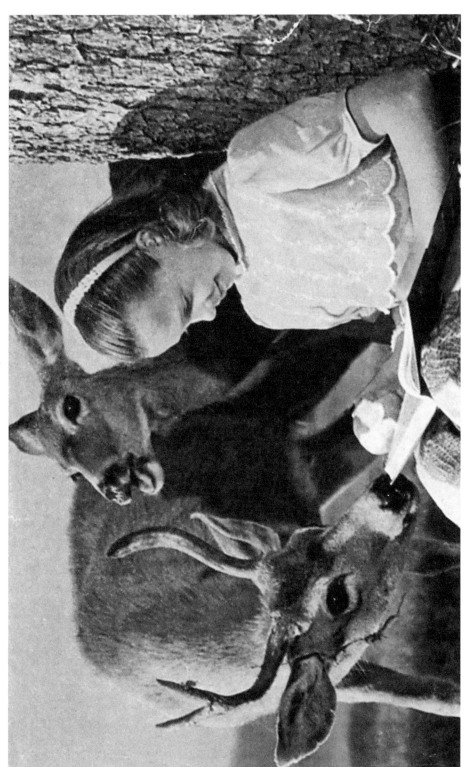

June Bartram and friends.

49

Chapter IV

SAN JUAN AVIATION & YACHTING ESTATES IS BORN

Technology changed the ways of business, not only automating maritime beacons but also some aspects of sawmill operations like the Spencer Mill. Eventually the remote location and the need for modernization caused the Spencer family to close down in 1942. With little else to provide an income to a Blakely resident, most people left the island for brighter prospects. The Spencer family sold the mill property and all of their Blakely Island holdings to Dr. Lloyd W. Hines and his wife Margaret in 1946. An Alaskan from the Aleutian Islands, Hines had left Alaska during World War II, fearing a Japanese invasion and harm to his family. His plans for Blakely Island were to develop it significantly in some manner that is unclear. Basically, the island slept through the ensuing decade, left to the animals and birds.

During the essential control of the island by the Spencers and the mill, one important historical blip occurred in the early 1920s. The State had certain lands reserved on Blakely. About 1922 the State Game Commission placed elk on Blakely Island and Cypress Island, four heifers and two bulls. According to an undated newspaper clipping in my files, the elk had been captured on the Hoh River, Clallam County, and held in Olympia for a time. They were trucked to Anacortes, where the truck was placed on a barge and delivered to Blakely by the fisheries steamer, *Elisha P. Ferry*. A motion picture cameraman went along to film the animals as they were liberated on the island. Because no predators existed on the island, the Commission assumed the animals would multiply fast. They did not. They died off, one by one, for unknown reasons. In a later writing Floyd Johnson said that a rumor that they swam off the islands and traveled all the way to Yakima was definitely untrue. Other than this brief residency and the domestic sheep, cows, and horses that once grazed there, the only animals known to be on the island have been deer, a few mice and squirrels, beach creatures such as otter, mink, recently harbor seals, and raccoons. The latter were numerous until about 1995, when a disease wiped out all of them. However, in 2005, residents have seen a few raccoons, which either swam here or had been hiding out in the interim.

By mid-century this island paradise called Blakely Island was rediscovered, in a sense. In 1953, Floyd Johnson, a sales person for a Cessna dealership in Portland, was the president of a pleasure flying club, Columbia Aviation Country Club. Together with a friend L.S. "Doc" White he searched the west coast from Canada to Mexico for a piece of property that could be developed as a private fly-in resort or second-home location for plane-owning friends. When his proposal to the club that they purchase property at Blakely was turned down, Floyd took a six-months option in July 1954 to purchase the entire 4900-acre island from Hines, with whom he was in a loose partnership for a brief time. Hines sold out his interests to Johnson March 15, 1957. Doc White acquired the old homestead cabin of Whitener. Curiously, this old cabin facing Obstruction later became the home of Chuck White, no relation, who built an addition to the picturesque place. When Chuck moved to the south end of the airstrip, the core cabin that once was Doc White's was preserved as a historical museum and sits under the fire bell near the north end of the airstrip.

Coincidentally, in 1956, Ernie and JoAnn Burkhart (author of this book) came from Los Angeles to vacation on Lopez Island with their two small children, Shelley and Scott, and cruised past Blakely Island's north end, then just a grassy clearing and forest. (In 1960 the couple negotiated with Floyd Johnson for purchase of the entire island and sent their lawyer from Los Angeles to investigate its practicality for them. They decided against the ambitious move and bought a lot, instead.)

In 1956, Floyd Johson faced a payment of $50,000-the balance of the purchase price ($60,000) for the island. Floyd and his wife Ola sold everything they owned, including properties in Florida, Michigan, and Portland-their latest home-to make the payment. The purchase price was only the beginning. The property had to be platted for lots, a water system developed to supply water to what I will subsequently call "the plat," the northwest end of the island where most homes are located, arrange for electrical power, and clear the heavily forested area for lots and facilities. Three miles of pipeline were required to bring water down from Horseshoe Lake and supply the plat from an interim storage tank situated part way down the mountainside. The loggers hacked out a crude air strip for access, the first Blakely Island airstrip of sorts. 80-year-old E.M. Graham from Shaw Island surveyed the land, sometimes paddling his own canoe over to Blakely.

Ola and Ole (as Floyd often was dubbed) soon lived in a Panabode that they enlarged (138). It was a hectic time for the Johnsons, because Floyd still flew back and forth to Portland to continue his job at the dealership. Ola stayed on the island alone, feverishly putting out pro-motional material and showing lots to prospective home owners, both pilots and boaters. Ola and her collie Tippy often were lonely. At that time today's marina did not exist. The Johnsons had installed a short boat ramp at their Panabode and a dock in front of the Blakely House. Ola told me that she would sit on the end of the dock and wave to any boats going by, just glad to see another human being.

A handful of pilots believed in the project and built the first homes of the development. They were: Chet Henson((42), Bob Adams(119), Jerry Pringle(136), Dr. Robert Greene (114), Dal Dallas (131), Purley Hamilton (162), Leo Kane (133), Jim Walthew, Don Fitzpatrick(14), Bill Beebe (24), Ed Merges(C), Robert Podhola (100). An important benefactor of the project was Cogs Campbell, a pilot 70+ years old, who offered to lend Floyd the money for the final payment due in 1956. Campbell also retained a very small property for his occasional use (144). Later residents knew when Cogs arrived on the island, for he flew his Cessna 310 like a fighter plane and tended to make a low pass over the air strip before landing. Although a fine pilot, Cogs was fierce-ly independent and refused ever to file a flight plan. Dal Dallas startled observers in a different way. He acquired an amphibious car, a model made in Germany. It looked like any other car, mostly like a Ford con-vertible. He got many belly laughs out of the unusual vehicle because, when he would drive the convertible down a boat ramp into the water, onlookers would galvanize into action screaming warnings and waving their arms. Their fright turned to amazement as the family chugged off toward Blakely or wherever.

Johnsons' promotional materials at the Troutdale Airport proved to be the key to luring Harold and Betty Bartram to Blakely Island, probably one of the most important factors in its development. In 1955 the Bartrams lived in Bend, Oregon, where they pursued a successful construction business. Harold flew a Piper Tri-Pacer and stopped at Troutdale to gas up. Intrigued by the pictures posted there of the new development at Blakely Island, the couple flew up there a few weeks later and bought lot 48 on the beach.

"At that time," said Harold, "most of the homes of the original owners were still under construction, and the air strip was really rough, just hacked out between the newly logged-off trees." Bartram and his business associate, Pete Sandford, jointly built a cabin to use as a second home. However, within the year, Sandford lost a close friend and business partner, decided to quit business, and dissolved his agreements with Bartram, first finishing up outstanding jobs. Bartram bought out his interest in the Blakely property.

By 1957, Harold Bartram and Floyd Johnson entered into a partnership agreement for development work and construction on Blakely Island. Each owned half of the commercial properties that included the restaurant, marina, and certain other activities. Before long, they terminated the partnership and had separate businesses with Bartram acquiring the shop and construction business, Floyd the commercial enterprises. Thereafter, Harold did development work, roads, airport improvement, water systems, and invoiced Johnson. He built homes under separate contracts with owners, almost 100 of the homes on the island over the next decades.

Floyd had hired three men to help. Ray Olson, who brought his family to live in a home made by joining two old cabins from Thatcher (52A), Neil Ogden, and George Lewis. Other early builders of the island who worked for either Floyd Johnson or Harold Bartram were: Sam Caruthers (Betty Bartram's brother, a carpenter who lived on the island with his family), H.B. "Herb" Reece (electrician, roofer, etc., also on the island), J.E. Harrison (carpenter), O.B. Senff (laborer),

Merton Christianson (carpenter), J.C. Stubbs (carpenter), J.R. Gusdahl (laborer), M.F. Hansen (laborer), S. Johnson (clearing land), C.C. Counch (clearing and road building), R.J. Adcock (laborer), J.C. Paris (laborer), I. Kjosen (carpenter), David Hogstedt (laborer), and Ned Gustan (clearing and road building).

In 1956 a careless transient camper started a beach fire at the southwest end of the plat, left without extinguishing it, and created a major fire that moved from the south end to the middle of the airstrip. Locals and a fledgling fire department worked frantically for 72 hours to contain it successfully. No doubt, every resident of the island was involved. Traces of burned trees can still be seen at the southwest edge of the airstrip. Another disaster, in an environmental sense, occurred in 1957, when a so-called wildcat logger capriciously removed logs at random and left residue that still is visible on the upper island forests. At this time, Floyd also realized that he needed additional capital if he were to be successful at the developing of a special island paradise. The island was just too big for one man to manage.

After extensive research in 1957 into the background of different timber companies, Floyd finally entered a highly unusual arrangement with Puget Sound Pulp & Timber Company (PSPTC) of Bellingham on August 27, 1957. He sold the bulk of the island, all the upland forests and its timber to PSPTC, retaining an easement to Floyd and Ola Johnson for use of those lands for recreational purposes that included the lakes, water, roads, etc. Johnson retained all shoreline back about 600 feet from Armitage Bay and Thatcher Bay and certain other pieces for future development. Such rights, of course, are subject to federal limits on waterfront lands, which permit public use up to the high tide mark on all beaches, PSPTC agreed not to harvest timber for a period of time, about 20 years.

Johnson realized that the development that he named San Juan Aviation & Yachting Estates (SJAYE) required some place for prospective buyers to stay and to eat. Blakely House Restaurant and the Skytel, a handsome Panabode structure, were built more or less concurrently between 1956 and 1958. The Skytel consisted of six lovely, large rooms with fireplaces that enjoyed a brisk patronage from visiting pilots, prospective lot owners, and homeowners' friends.

Floyd purchased two 51-foot war surplus housing units at Seattle and barged them to create Blakely House Restaurant. It took shape under the management of George and Alice Johnson of Bellingham, Washington. In the 1950s Floyd had frequented the Johnsons' small restaurant on State Street and, impressed with the food, he persuaded them to move to Blakely. The Johnsons became much beloved, both for their warmth and for their outstanding food. Their strawberry pie was legendary for patrons, and Kerry and Dick Demers remember fondly the onion bread served with dinners. The operation consisted of the second floor restaurant and a full and roomy bar, the Peavine Room, at the southeast end of the building. Entry was from a deck fronting on the water. Shortly thereafter Rosemary Lind opened a well-stocked gift shop called "On The Isle" below the restaurant.

George and Alice received their groceries from a delivery truck at Obstruction Pass. Deliveries of anything could be adventurous. Around 1960 Bartram had a boom truck and trailer en route to Blakely, plus restaurant equipment for George Johnson loaded on the makeshift raft powered by an outboard that was used for transport. Between Obstruction Pass and Blakely in rough water off Obstruction Island, the motor quit. The raft grounded on Obstruction, was holed by bouncing on a rock, and flooded. It listed and rolled the whole boom truck and trailer off into the water and partly on the beach. The men aboard hurriedly took most of George's equipment off to higher ground.

Bartram said, "We had a dredge was on Blakely Island working on the marina. We got the operators to hook onto the raft by a chain that was just out of the water. It rolled again and then we had to get a scuba diver to attach another chain. Finally we got hooked up, and the dredge lifted the whole thing to set it on the beach in front of our house. The speedometer and headlights were half full of water. We drained the boom truck motor and other parts and dried them out. Then we put diesel in to clear it out. We used the truck for years thereafter with no trouble. Incidentally, George's equipment was okay."

.

Bartram had his hands full with physically creating order from chaos. Here's how the terrain looked at this pivotal time: Visualize no landfill, no solid ground at all where the marina is now located, just a shoreline that ran along today's marina parking lot Water extended to Driftwood

Beach. From the shore road a long dock extended toward Peavine Pass west of and roughly parallel to today's marina building. It extended to a point about where the gas dock is today. No land there, no rocks, no channel into the marina, just water. Beginning about where the present dock is attached to land one could enter a narrow channel that went westerly inside the present beach in front of owners Foster, Keyes, Weller, etc. One could have rowed a dinghy almost to Blakely House.

One of Bartram's earliest projects was to fill in that channel and create a berm (now the beach) to keep out the ocean. Even so, extremely high tides occasionally caused salt water to come into the front yards of the beach front home owners. It took two years for Bartram's crew to dredge out the marina and use the material to create the land on which the store is located.

The dredging process was interesting. and time-consuming. Bartram employee, Sam Caruthers, said they used a two-drum donkey with V8 Cadillac army surplus tank engine. The first setup was from where today's marina store is located to the beginning of settlement road entrance. When time came to breach the beach to create the present marina entrance, the crew put the donkey dredge on the original Blakely ferry. Caruthers went on,

> Next was to establish a tail hold out in Peavine Pass. At
> first we used a track off a bulldozer, but that was lost
> when the attached cable broke. A reefnetter suggested
> that we use a large boulder. We selected one in front of
> the restaurant, drilled a hole in it, and-at the first high tide
> lifted it up from the stern of the old ferry and dragged it
> into position out toward Peavine.for our tail hold. That
> was a big success, and we used it to complete the channel
> dredging. After we were done, we brought the boulder up
> again and stored it under the deck of the present marina
> boat ramp. The donkey was sold to Del Taylor, who sold
> it to a Port Orchard log shipping operation.

When the fill was completed to create the present marina site, which largely consisted of boulders, the workers installed pilings near the entrance to mark the southwesterly edge of the channel and help to control the tidal currents that made entering the marina dicey during strong currents and winds. Once the landfill was completed and settled Bartram constructed a building and office for management of the new marina slip rentals and provide basic grocery supplies for visitors and owners.

The entrance pilings rotted out and, in 1982, Bartram and then employee Don Burkhart removed the pilings and replaced them with riprap to create a genuine breakwater. After Pete Taggares acquired the point called Blakely Head, the peninsula across from today's marina, more dredging deepened the east end of the marina to allow boat dockage directly from the peninsula for Taggares. The rest of the lagoon was filled in with the residue as allegedly a more aesthetic site, but others remember the marshy area fondly as a lovely tidal estuary. Afterwards some pilots eye the filled area as a possible emergency landing place for errant take-offs-surely not the best but not many other choices exist, either, just water, mountains, rocks. Fortunately, it never had to be used as such.

The next or concurrent important project after the marina landfill was to upgrade the airport. It merely had been graded with a bulldozer and followed the rolling terrain, about half as wide as the 2005 version. At the south end was a swale that attracted standing water during rain. Bartram's crew graded it better with a bulldozer and scraper to level out the dips. The south end required five feet of land fill and the north end seven feet of fill. To this day, despite several more improvements and paving, it still has a rise in the middle that makes it impossible to see a plane standing at opposite ends of the airport.

Although not the fault of the emerging airstrip, a severe accident occurred July 17, 1959. Pioneer homeowners Dal and Hazel Dallas in a twin-engine aircraft new to them landed slightly before the north end of the airstrip. Dal "poured on the coal" and one engine quit, causing them to veer off the airstrip into the forest. The plane caught fire. Dal got his back seat passengers out instantly, but the delay meant he and Hazel were caught in the blaze and were burned badly. The burning plane spread into the trees and resulted in the cleared area that Blakelyites call the corridor, where hangars have been constructed. However, the couple recovered fully and returned with a single engine plane.

Bartram and Johnson's development efforts at this stage resulted in entire rafts of logs, which were hauled to the Orcas mill, sawed into building lumber, and returned to Blakely for use. "We rented a barge *Nordland* at first to haul materials on and off the island. [The *Nordland* served those few residents on Indian Island near Port Townsend in the early 2000s.] Then I built my own barge and ran it with a 25-30 HP motor," said Harold. One traveler to the island by barge they called Packit was a horse for the Bartram children, an ex-racehorse because a horseman told Harold that they were the safest due to constant handling. It was true; the horse named Vance put up with the most inexperienced equestrian. Doug Bartram, the eldest child, was the most enthusiastic and skilled rider. In 2005 Kaleeha, Lance Douglas's horse, lives at the pasture above Horseshoe Lake, no doubt as lonely as Doug's steed.

When the Bartrams had moved onto the island in 1957 their four children were only ages 2-12. Harold hired part-time construction personnel as needed plus Sam Caruthers and Herb Reece as full-time employees, and each had children. The Olsons still lived on the island for a time. The old Thatcher School was long inactive. The school-age children had to attend classes on Orcas Island. Thus, each morning about 7:30 all 10 or 12 school children boarded the Bartrams' 26-foot boat for Obstruction Pass on Orcas Island to catch the school bus, returning the same way around 4:30 p.m. The children were: Doug, Mike, June, and Jack Bartram, Pam, Janet, Billy, Debby and Dick Reece, Judy "Button" Olson, and Cindy Caruthers. The marina did not exist; Harold Bartram or an employee rowed the children to the moored boat.

June Bartram was only in first grade when the family began the school run. She said it was a bit frightening. On foggy mornings when the boat crept along, she felt as if they were the only people in the world. At Orcas Island along Obstruction Pass about a half mile from the current resort Harold Bartram anchored a float in deep water. From shore to the float he placed a boardwalk with rope hand rails across two large logs. For the return trip the children were told not to go beyond the first log until the boat was docked, because the wake caused the second log and float to bob up and down. Possibly the action would cause a child to fall into the water.

No one did fall in until one day an adult couple came to board the boat for a visit to Doc Taylor on Blakely. The woman went out to the float, and June said, "As she was an adult, we did not think we should tell her not to go." In fact, the children started to follow her. The boat's wake did upset their balances, causing the woman and several children to fall into the water. All got out safely, although some were in deep water. It was a cold and wet lot that completed the trip to Blakely-- especially the woman clad in a dress.

June said that a bachelor settler near the makeshift dock came to help everyone and teased her because she had seaweed in her mouth when she got to shore. She affectionately remembers the man, Jack Hanson, because he was a self-appointed guardian of the children as they came and went and waited for the school bus. In fact, later he inherited Armitage Island, frequently visited the Bartram family, and wanted the children to call him "Grandpa."

Actually, in this watery San Juan County, they were not the only students attending the Orcas Schools by boat. Usually the trips were fairly serene, as the waters between the islands are somewhat protected. However, on the afternoon of the 1962 Columbus Day hurricane the waves were running six feet high and breaking over the bow of the boat when Harold retrieved the children from Obstruction Pass. "When I think of it now," Betty Bartram said, "this was crazy. Surely the kids could have stayed with someone on Orcas over night."

Other islands had similar arrangements for school age children. High school students played football and basketball against other island schools, e.g., Orcas High teams went on the tugboat belonging to a different island resident to play against Lopez High School (Mike played football, Doug basketball). The tug hauled the teams, parents, and fans to the games, waited for them, and took them back to Orcas again. Bartrams remember these trips as an ongoing party time, with everyone crammed below deck having cookies and soft drinks or cocoa, bundled up against the weather in winter. One of the Shaw students became a lifelong friend of June Bartram from such encounters. Truly it was a world away from the average school experience.

At Blakely, Bartram's crews were involved in building roads, as well as dredging. To achieve this, they built a sort of sled with an A-frame device and winch to pull out stumps, which they dragged out of the way to burn. When Harold was clearing with a large bulldozer the area now called the corridor, one four-feet-diameter stump surrounded by rock refused to move. "No problem," said Harold later. "I just used dynamite. I flew many cases of dynamite to the island in my Piper Tri-Pacer. Well, I guess I used a mite too much dynamite on that stump. When it blew, Lee Hoffman (36) discovered a big rock had come right through the roof of his new house's garage and almost hit his Land Rover. The vehicle was not damaged, though."

Even more urgent was drastic improvement to the water system from Horseshoe Lake to the settlement. At that time part way downhill was a wooden water tank with a parachute over it for a roof. A 1-1/2" poly-ethylene pipe led from the lake to the tank, just lying on the ground. The pump was a 3 HP Briggs & Stratton unit. "We used to start it up and just let it run until it ran out of gas, which pumped sufficient water to fill the tank.

"This tank held about 1,000 gallons," said Harold. In 1962 the crew constructed a 2500-gallon concrete tank, although the pump still sat in the open and the pipes were above ground. They electrified the pump by running wires from tree to tree, starting at the settlement with a transformer at the bottom to step up the power and another at the top to step it down again. Today the electric lines just lie on the ground, two 50,000 gallon tanks furnish water for the settlement, and the pump is in its house. Actually, when the Orcas Power Company installed the power loop that encircles the islands, electricity was routed down to the pump house directly from the lines above.

At a special meeting in 1961 the owners of lots in the San Juan Aviation Estates agreed to form the Blakely Island Maintenance Commission. They drew up Articles of Association that declared that one had to be a member in order to own property, and could not own property without being a member, that only members were entitled to use the BIMC properties and facilities, and that each property would pay a yearly fee to cover the community expenses. The largest of these were for the water system, roads and airport maintenance. The board members of the Commission are volunteers and change regularly according to a predetermined schedule. Ever since 1961, this board has been the guide for decisions affecting community properties. Certainly the board discussions and annual meetings have been lively, even noisy and argumentative at times, but the volunteer management of most factors has continued to prevail over contentions of various types. A few lawsuits have arisen and were resolved. Reasonable rules of conduct for owners and families have been drawn up, amended now and then, and largely observed by all.

Certain restrictions on building and activities were filed, most of which are not of interest to the casual reader. The restrictions did include such matters as prohibiting manufactured homes, leaving trailers or motorhomes on the owners' properties, the necessity of completing at least the exterior of a building within a reasonable time after start of construction, a minimum square footage for homes, and other matters designed to maintain a neat and upscale appearance to the development. Each home owner was to be approved by the Blakely Maintenance Commission and to receive a membership certificate. My family (114) holds Certificate No. 19 dated November 17, 1961, and still owns the home on Blakely then purchased from the original builder, Dr. Robert Greene of Oregon. A letter to the members from Floyd Johnson dated May 4, 1960, indicates that members at that time were considering construction of a swimming pool with dressing rooms and facilities. Nothing ever came of this. The only pools at the island were that of Jerry Pringle (136), now covered, and an indoor pool at Dick Sutton's home (89).

In 1962 the Johnsons were able to start planning their dream home at the south end of the airstrip facing Lopez and Orcas islands and began construction in 1963. From an article by Herb Belanger in the Seattle Times of November 15, 1964, "...Throughout, the house is finished in antique-elm prefinished paneling. The ceilings all are open beam and all are at different angles, producing an unusual spacious effect." And "The Johnson home is in reality two houses spread under a rectangular roof, and has four covered patios, dominated by translucent cutouts in the roof." The home (13) has polished native stones set in cement at the entry. I remember Ola Johnson's unusual bathroom counters with sea creatures and shells set into transparent plastic, and the enclosed private garden visible through a ceiling to floor window from the main bathroom.

From the beginning of the development a few islanders have constructed rather streamlined, narrow log rafts on Spencer Lake, powered by low-H.P. outboard motors. Possibly the S.S. Ola was the very first one in 1958. Owners and friends typically brought a picnic lunch aboard, motored to the center of the lake, jumped off to swim and climbed back on the raft, sang, or just enjoyed the Tom Sawyer style of life, the wild forest scenery and the birds. To this day a handful of owners continue this carefree practice.

Among the owners or offspring in 1962, an arbitrary cut-off time, who still have homes on Blakely Island in 2005 are: Don Fitzpatrick, Don Douglas, Ernie Burkhart, Andrew Galbraith, Bob Adams, Cogs Campbell, Doug Moreton, Bob Rankin, Bob Lynch, Del Taylor, Bob Foster, Roger Baird, Dr. Charlie Mills, Harold Bartram, and David Strausz.

Blakely airstrip in 1960's before paving.

THE GIANT BELLOWS which hangs above fireplace in the Floyd Johnson home on Blakely Island goes far back In San Juan history. It once was used in an early lumber mill at Thatcher, a pioneer island village now deserted. Shown above are, lef to right, standing, Mr. Johnson, Les Gormley, Seattle flyer who will soon build a summer home on the island, Mrs. Johnson and Mrs. Eva Dorenwendt. Seated is Miss Kathy Underwood, a Spokane model who has been vacationing on the "isle of flyers."

—(Post-Intelligencer Photo by John M. "Hock" Miller.)

July 3rd, 1961. Courtesy of Seattle Post-Intelligencer

The original clubhouse was the scene of merry times and good food for Blakely residents and visitors after it became Blakely House.

George and Alice Johnson, operators of Blakely House Restaurant, with Santa from the Christmas ship. Courtesy of Betty Bartram.

Richard Hiss (right) was the first operator of Blakely Marina. He had a Union Oil Company "76" franchise. Courtesy of Seventy-six Magazine.

Bayliss Harriss (R) chats with an Island Sky Ferries pilot.

For awhile after Spencer Lake washed out, a major waterfall existed at sawdust beach. Young Don Burkhart watches.

Crazybuck, also called Scarbuck and Starbuck, was a tame four-point buck that often came up on the deck of Blakely House. Sketch by Frederick Hubbard.

Horseshoe cabin about 1978, before it was remodled.

Ernie Burkhart and children, a typical Blakely family of the 1970's.

Denise Burkhart and friends sort shells and sea creatures, a typical pastime for Blakely kids.

Cyclist threads his way through foxgloves on a Blakely trail.

Walt Van Wagenen taxis toward the airstrip from his hangar across from the former Blakely House. Entrance Mountain on Orcas Island is in the background.

Blakely kids and tame deer in 1961. Coutresy of Steve Wilson and Cascade Magazine.

Harold Bartram in front of the unpaved airstrip.

The "Pack-It" delivers a vehicle to Blakely.

"A summit meeting."
Don Fitzpatrick, Eva Gormley, Andy & Phyllis Galbraith, Paula Douglas and Margaret Alley.

Hand feeding the island deer.

Stu Knopp, Carnegie Medal Winner. Sketch by Frederick L. Hubbard.

Dear Mr. Knopp:

I want To Thank you for geting Me out of The water.

Thank you for The Kangaroo. It was a Kute Kangaroo. Julie has a Kangaroo Just like it. I Think you are a nice Man

Thank you

Form Jennifer

Jennifer Lewis penned her thanks to Knopp for saving her life.

Chapter V
ALL THINGS GOOD AND BAD

For the first dozen years of SJAYE, the population of Blakely was so small that everyone was well-acquainted. Parties broke out for almost any occasion, often held at the Clubhouse, as the building for Blakely House Restaurant was called initially. Older residents remember lively events in what is now the Meslins' living room, e.g., a limbo dance contest one Christmas week. Herb Reece, well over six feet tall and thin as a bean pole, won with a pass-through surely not higher than 40 inches. He was bent back practically horizontal, walking forward with knees bent. Any resident present during the Christmas and New Year's holidays was welcome at these lively events.

During those years of traditional families many wives and children lived on the island full time in summer, while their husbands flew in for weekends or vacation time. For three years I, a Los Angeles resident, spent June to September on the island with four children, a dog, cat, and-while Denise was a baby and the oldest Burkhart was 10--the family sitter as well-all in our small Panabode cabin. While watching small children Paula Douglas, JoAnn Burkhart, Jane Pringle, and either Priscilla Gardner or Phyllis Galbraith regularly played bridge. At least three children and I took our 14-foot runabout to Obstruction Pass dock, then drove to Eastsound for groceries and incidentals. Floyd Johnson called me "Fearless Fosdick" for these voyages.

As more and more homeowners spent weeks or months at Blakely Island and looked for excitement, the islanders became pranksters. All ages. For instance Nancy Fitzpatrick and Marilyn Moreton put live toads in the Fitzes bathroom during their parents' dinner party

A teenage boy couldn't resist ringing the fire bell one day, a prank that was poorly received, to say the least. Sam Caruthers made points with the youngsters with a "Candy Man" sign on his truck and the candy to prove it. Surprisingly, no children ever have wandered away to become hopelessly lost., although several islanders searched for hours one afternoon for two boys, Lance and Don, ages 7 and 5, only to have them saunter home unfazed as darkness fell. The lads had just been exploring the forest and "knew where we were."

The adults were creative in their pranks and divided themselves into the south enders (south end of airstrip) and the north enders-the Confederates and the Union armies. The loosely unwritten rules went something like this: on any dark, not necessarily stormy night one "army" or the other got the inspiration to stealthily invade the other's territory. Residents peacefully watching television or half-sleeping about 10:00 p.m. would be awakened to the roar of Dick Alley's toy cannon and other racket by the invading group. The invadees were required by custom to then open their homes to food and spirits for an impromptu party. In 1962 Margaret and Ed Merges dressed in Confederate uniforms, Bill and Ida Beebe, and Betty and Don Fitzpatrick invaded the north or Yankee end of the island during an unidentified owner's dinner party to honor George Wilson, according to an old Blakely Log or newsletter put out by the Johnsons.

About 1962 cabin owner Bill Jones (117) and his brand new bride Nada had just retired for their first night, when revelers decided to give them an old-fashioned charivari (shivaree). A dozen or so neighbors approached the darkened home and suddenly beat on pans, shot off the Alley cannon, and gleefully made noise. The Jones eventually appeared, fully clothed but with understandably skeptical expressions, and reluctantly invited the obnoxious ones into the house for cake and coffee. This quaint custom was inflicted on the newly married Phyllis (Galbraith) and Joe Strosahl, as well.

Despite the fact that most plane owners were in comfortable circum-stances, on Blakely all residents were deemed equal in the "people sanc-tuary," as Ola Johnson dubbed the island. Most preferred to build mod-est but often somewhat unusual cabins. George Wilson, an Eastern Oregon wheat rancher, built an octagonal house (19), 46 feet in diameter, on a platform 58 feet in diameter. The floor was supported by eight 4-by-16-inch beams that rested on eight rubber-tired plastic wheels set on a track in a circular cement trough. Necessarily all connections had to be flexible At the touch of a button to a 3/4 horsepower motor the platform revolved on tracks about 320 degrees, facing sun, shade, sea or forest as desired. It faced "Half-swacked Bay," as the former loggers had dubbed the long, sandy south beach. George insisted the home was not just a toy but a practical solution to seeking sunshine during the winter months, the times when a wheat rancher is able to vacation at Blakely.

Pranksters couldn't resist kidding genial George. He awoke one morning to find that, when he punched a button to make his house revolve, a makeshift outhouse on roller skates was moving along with it. Inside was a mannequin dressed in a bikini. Speaking of outhouses, Martha Mills (Galbraith) and sister Barbara built their own before their parents had a home or bathroom. Martha said they dug a shallow hole and built a small frame around it. Dense forest prevented passers-by from seeing occupants.

Another unusual home was the four-story, narrow chalet of Lee Hoffman (36) that seemed plucked from Austria. Inventive Zan Strausz, siblings and friends, built their own South Seas style structure on the southwest spit (near Rogich). It was a creative three-story structure made of miscellaneous boards and reeds with a thatched roof. No one seems to know what happened to it. Don Spawn, now Rogich site, dwelled in solitary splendor at the extreme end of South Beach (south of airstrip) on a spit of sand. If a tidal wave ever showed up in the our north Sound, would it still be there?

John Hill (22) decided to name the island roads. The marina road was Dockside, the perimeter road Surfside, the main road to the lake Upside, the Blakely Peak Road Topside, the road to the then garbage dump uphill from Horseshoe Lake was Offside, and a trail was named Backside.

Otters were too-frequent visitors to the residents at the south end of the airstrip. The Mills family had to oust a family from living under their house, because the odor was awful (otters spray when disturbed), and Bill Beebe put up a sign for awhile "Otter Crest Bed & Breakfast" because of his unwanted guests.

In 1962 the Blakely Marina was completely renovated. The building size was doubled, the laundry facilities expanded, lighted floats installed. The area was landscaped and a barbecue facility and picnic area created. The marina was leased to Richard Hiss, formerly a mechanical engineer at Hughes Aircraft in Los Angeles, who built the expanded building with his own funds. He was an official Union 76 distributor. Next came Bayliss and Tressa Harriss ("Pappy and Dude"), assisted by Dutch and Olive Schulz. Bayliss was a California transplant and avid mariner, who moored his lovely Newporter Debutante, a sleek motor sailer, in the marina. He was something of a party guy but a fine yachtsman. Tales of Bayliss's escapades abound from the older islanders. Harriss enjoyed sailing to Friday Harbor for an evening out. In 1971 he died there by choking on a piece of steak.

The Blakely House Restaurant became extremely popular with flyers and boaters. The Peavine Room adjacent to the dining room overflowed each night and attracted celebrities, as well as locals. The Brothers Four often came to Blakely and sometimes would perform there, just for fun. They made friendly connections and, in 2005, were back at Blakely entertaining once more at Ken Parker's lot.

Other entertainment included Scarbuck or Crazybuck, as he was variously called, a magnificent four-point buck that came up the steps onto the restaurant deck to peek in the windows at startled diners. He just liked people. Even though residents were discouraged from feeding him, he would stick his head into the windows of cabins just to schmooz. When my family had a batch of kittens born on the island, Crazybuck was fascinated by them and tried to lick them like a cat. The kittens were totally unappreciative of the gesture. Unfortunately, a resident's dog chased the buck into the bay one day. He tried to swim across the currents of Peavine Pass to Obstruction Island but drowned.

Throughout the years at SJAYE, a boat trip to the Rosario Resort on Orcas Island for a Sunday brunch or romantic summer evening dinner has been a treat for Blakely residents-an occasional change from dining at Blakely House. From Blakely's northwest shore the white building stands out against a backdrop of trees and mountains. Rosario was built by Seattle ship-building magnate Robert Moran in 1909 as a retreat for himself and his family and friends, following the news from his doctor that he would die soon unless he adopted a more healthful lifestyle. The structure reflects ship's architecture in its interior finishing, the massive stairway railings, and sturdy construction with 12 inch walls and 7/8 inch plate glass windows. Moran loved to play the organ and installed a 1872 pipe Aeolian organ in the mezzanine of the home, often playing concerts before breakfast to awaken his guests. He refuted his doctor's dire warning and lived on for decades at Orcas Island. Today the stunning resort and spa has expanded to serve guests but stands like the fabled rock of Gibralter on a rocky shore facing Blakely. It even has a Blakely room.

Rosemary Lind in her gift shop below Blakely House was horrified on August 9, 1962, to see the Cessna 210 of Ernie and JoAnn Burkhart approach the north end of the airstrip all too quietly and all too low. Its tail hit the beach between Blakely House and the Johnson residence, slamming the fuselage onto the ground to skid through a large log. Later Lind said, "I didn't come out, because I was sure they were dead and I didn't want to look at them."

Injured we were but very much alive. Leaving our four children with a sitter, we flew to Friday Harbor for groceries. On the return trip we detoured to fly over Mount Constitution to sightsee, then turned to descend toward Blakely over Point Lawrence. At about 2,500 feet it was necessary to lose altitude, so Ernie put the 210 into a sideslip. The plane had extended range tanks, the gas slid out toward the wingtip (even though the tanks were one-third full) and, when Ernie straightened up the plane, the engine would not start. We rode the plane down under good control but simply ran out of space. We slid through a huge log that Floyd Johnson had just placed there between our departure and dramatic return to protect newly planted grass from vehicles, almost turned over, and settled back down.

Ernie was badly injured with both legs broken and a large cut within his mouth; I sustained a blow to my head which blackened and almost closed both eyes and sustained a shoulder bruise from a flying king-sized jar of peanut butter, but both of us survived and were flown to Bellingham's hospital. The FAA investigators found that the Cessna 210's strainer drain cable had been installed at the factory on the wrong side of the intake manifold. It finally sawed through the manifold wall and allowed too much air to the mixture for the fuel injection engine. That's why it did not start, and we recalled that it had been hard to start on the ground earlier. The last we saw of that airplane was on a truck leaving Blakely on a barge.

In proof of the saying that bad things happen in threes, Ernie went flying at Santa Monica (the family still lived in Los Angeles in 1962) before one of his casts was off. The rented plane suddenly went into full prop pitch over Santa Monica Bay (some part had broken), and he had to declare an emergency landing although without incident. About two weeks later he bogged down his jeep near Driftwood Beach on Blakely, got out with his cast and crutches, fell down in the mud, and half the island was involved to rescue him and the jeep.

Less dramatic, to be sure, were the every day events of the island. In 1962 Floyd and Ola Johnson published the Blakely Island Log, a newsletter sent to all home owners. In 1963 sixty homes existed on the island. From the Log we learned that the Rankin children kept falling out of their sleeping loft, that the 30th wedding anniversary of Margaret and Dick Alley (116) found Dick drinking champagne out of a slipper, and that in 1962 the ladies of the island had a Meet 'n Eat Club lunch each Wednesday at Blakely House.

In 1962 several owners suggested the establishment of game birds on the island and the formation of a private hunting club. At the time it was suggested that a fishing club entity also be formed to take advantage of the lake's bounty. Members were to be limited to three to five guests per year for fishing. Neither of these proposals came to pass. Instead, over the years owners whose families do fish the lakes have been asked for donations. Horseshoe Lake has been stocked regularly with as many as 20,000 trout fingerlings. Chief volunteers in monitoring this program were Ed Merges (C) and Bill Beebe. The fishing program and tennis court maintenance (also a donation situation then) became incorporated into the responsibilities of BIMC for the good of all. Guests are still to be limited, however. In the early days of SJAYE outboard motors were allowed on Horseshoe Lake, and water skiing was popular. Before long residents encouraged boaters to use only electric motors and not gas engines. Finally the latter were banned entirely.

During a dark and stormy night residents, mostly absent for the winter months, were startled to learn that on January 30, 1965, much of Spencer Lake washed out into Thatcher Bay in spectacular fashion, viewed and reported by passengers aboard a ferry bound for Lopez. According to them, a torrent of water, trees, and the remains of the old Thatcher mill and post office building surged into the sea. The small retaining dam had collapsed under the weight of melting snow, heavy rain and high water and, like pulling a plug in a bath tub, roared down the ravine, leaving Spencer Lake's level at half mast. Blakely Marina's Bayliss Harriss wrote for the Friday Harbor Journal:

> The break created a ravine estimated at an increase of
> approximately 75 feet deeper than the former run-off
> stream bed. Both Thatcher and Eastsound were muddy
> for miles in all directions. Hundreds of trees and litter
> covered an area of approximately 30 square miles, con-
> sisting of various trees, the old Thatcher Mill site, which
> was completely demolished, and fruit trees and their
> products floated everywhere throughout the Eastsound
> area, Peavine and Obstruction Pass.

By 4:00 p.m. on the 31st the ravine was cut to bare rock. In the process the runoff created a fine waterfall that dropped into a tranquil pool thereafter like a South Seas destination. The force of the water was so huge that it moved iron machinery from the remains of the old mill several feet to the sawdust beach and the bay itself. The heavy Pelton wheel was moved into the bay, where it still may be seen at low tide. The original Thatcher post office was decimated, leaving Blakelyites with only memories of visiting the funky remains with its 30-degree tilted floors and walls. No doubt, thousands of amazed bass that populate Spencer Lake found themselves in salt water, as well. The dam was replaced; indeed, it is now the road to the south end of the island from a point above the bay. The 70-acre lake gradually filled to its regular level.

Such heart-stopping drama could occur any ordinary day. One fine summer afternoon, July 25, 1965, Stuart Knopp (38) was painting his deck facing Eastsound. His son Leon was outside, saw a child fall off a power cruiser just off the shore, and yelled for his father. The boat continued toward the marina, even as Stu-never thinking about his own safety-shouted to Don Douglas next door, plunged down the steep bank, and dove into the chilly water. The child's parka kept her afloat for few seconds, but she had gone under water twice before Stu reached her. Towing the hysterical child at arm's length, he swam back toward shore 75-100 yards away. Meanwhile, Douglas had reached the water and waded in to help if he were needed. Teeth chattering and spent from the exertion and cold Stu dragged himself on shore and collapsed to catch his breath. Douglas comforted the child and, once he knew that Knopp was okay, started up the bank to get blankets for them both. After the rescuer and rescued were stabilized, he called the marina. There the parents, Yakima friends of islanders Rankin and Lynch, were milling around in shock after they realized-only after they docked--that their daughter, Jennifer Lewis, was missing and that she had taken off her life jacket. One can imagine that sinking feeling and the subsequent joy they felt when the telephone call came in to say she was safe. For his heroism Stu Knopp was awarded the Carnegie Medical later. Only then did residents learn that he also had received both the Distinguished Flying Cross and the Air Medal during his service in World War II and the Korean War...truly a hero.

Children and adults alike have been thoroughly brainwashed about the dangers of any smoking and fireworks up island, and island juveniles deserve praise for heeding the warnings. In fact, in an age of criticism of juvenile behavior, one must be proud of the Blakely Island children, who impress upon their peers that it is definitely not "cool" to throw wrappers and garbage along trails and roads, either, and are known to pick up the occasional trash that has escaped from passing vehicles. Children have obeyed more regularly than adults the very firm edict about not walking across the runway...ever. The hazards of speeding on the small motorcycles so popular on Blakely are emphasized.

Tragedy struck, however, one summer day in the 1970s. One child was killed, the other injured on the road between the marina and Driftwood Beach. They were offspring of a visitor to an islander's home. He had schooled the children on the basics of riding small motorcycles, then told them firmly to go no farther than the hill between the air strip and the marina. BEING children they could not resist going farther and faster. Ascending the steep hill toward

Driftwood they turned the blind corner and ran head on into a virtually stopped jeep driven by an islander and were thrown from the cycles. One fetched up against a tree and died. The other was injured but recovered. All residents were devastated by the incident.

In 1967, the aging but much loved George and Alice Johnson ceased management of the Blakely House Restaurant and turned it over to Bruce and Marjorie Anderson and their two popular teen-age daughters. George and Alice lived near Floyd Johnson's home for a few years, then retired to the mainland in 1971. However, the Andersons wanted to close in 1971, and Floyd decided not to reopen the restaurant. Its popularity had made it a place that attracted too many outsiders and was noisy, negating the ambiance of the island.

The restaurant building became the private residence of Ed Hostman and later Jacques Meslin and family. By the way, Ed Hostman had an unusual problem with the house. Due to erroneous information Hostman proceeded to plug an abandoned drain pipe in the accepted fashion, i.e., stuff a wad of newspaper down the pipe and seal it with concrete. Unfortunately, no one told him about needing newspaper. He poured considerable concrete down the pipe that just kept on going and plugged up his entire drainage system. He had to go clear through the slab to get things working properly, and to this day Meslins still have mysterious problems with drainage here and there

Roy Franklin was the guiding forcebehind the success of Island Sky Ferries and San Juan Airlines. Credit to Hugh Stratford, Photographer.

Bill Booze, pilot

Dr. Malcolm Heath was a legendary island doctor for San Juan Islands residents. Courtesy of Seattle Post-Intelligencer, March 8, 1964, page12.

Bob Nichols, pilot

The San Juan Islands air services landed pretty much anywhere in the early days.

Chapter VI
FLEDGLING AIR SERVICES

Blakely primarily was and is a pilots' island. The air services that served the islands have always been an integral necessity, as well, one means for islanders and their guests to access the island. The first airstrip, as indicated earlier, was not much more than a bulldozed track across the island. With some drainage and smoothing it became an adequate grass strip. Originally it was 2,100 feet but the south end overrun extends it a bit more A high place in the center of the strip makes it impossible to see the opposite end; thus, the requirement was initiated that pilots first taxi to about the center portion to check for other planes on the strip Of course, a UNICOM provision also helped. An Eastsound wind coming down from the northwest strikes the runway at a 90-degree angle and separates to sweep around both ends. Thus, the wind-socks at either end sometimes indicate different wind directions. The southeast winds create difficult turbulence for pilots on final approach. All this has always made life interesting for landing watchers. Even though the airport is excellent, Blakely-ites are wary of such conditions. The saga of air service to the islands is part of Blakely's history, too.

The first scheduled air service to serve the San Juan Islands was a one-plane (a red Stinson four-seat Voyager), one-pilot (Bob Schoen) affair out of Orcas that began service in 1947 as Orcas Island Air Service, becoming one of the oldest commuter airlines in the United States. From makeshift and challenging airstrips in the islands the service transported people to and from Bellingham, where an air service, Western Washington Aircraft, operated. Schoen provided an incredibly old (even for that time) Whippet automobile to bring passengers to and from Bellingham's Leopold Hotel. There the owner/manager John

Pierce accommodated Schoen by taking messages and making reservations like a pseudo-office of Orcas Island Air Service. A year later the company renamed Island Sky Ferries added a second plane and pilot Roy Franklin.

Franklin tells of one of his earlier flights for Schoen from Eastsound to Waldron Island. "We had wooden props on the plane in those days," he said. "On takeoff a big Chinese pheasant flew up and connected with the prop. With the pheasant's remains all over the plane and windshield we still were able to continue and land again to check the plane. We thought the prop was OK but played it safe and headed for Friday Harbor for a thorough checkout."

Over Crane Island the plane began to shake violently after the tip of the prop flew off, and the engine started smoking and stopped. No field was within reach from 800 feet altitude. With incredible good luck and skill Franklin managed to insert the plane, wings vertical, between two tall firs, straighten up and make almost a perfect landing in a tiny field. He laughs today to remember that a home owner adjacent to the field was working in her garden, turned around and "jumped five feet in the air" at the sight of his plane-his landing had been so quiet and she was upwind from the site.

Flying the islands at that time certainly required bush pilot skills. A short airstrip at Orcas, not far from the ferry landing, was surrounded by trees--merely a grassy field and short, making landings and takeoffs memorable. If Franklin had to make a night flight to Eastsound, he literally could not see that airport at all until Virginia Ferris, co-operator of the field, put out old highway flares, wicks burning diesel oil in steel containers, on the left side of the runway to guide Schoen's planes. The same was true of Lopez Island and, even worse, it had no airport at all for several years and the pilots used various farm fields as needed. Friday Harbor's airport was just a square, rough field, really a cow pasture, where the planes landed diagonally to maximize runway length...but by gosh, the air service used it! Roy Franklin hit a cow one time on landing but sustained no injuries to passengers.

Things did not improve very soon. Well into the 1960s, maybe even 1970s, Shaw Island's strip crossed a road meant for autos and ran under a set of wires midway. Lopez Island was a little better; yet a plane carrying two professional pilots and their wives hit a deer on takeoff. They lifted off enough so the wheels did not hit the deer, but the horizontal stabilizer did and downed the plane, killing all four people. Waldron Island's original strip ran southeast-northwest uphill between tall trees. The second one had a dogleg in the runway, which was eliminated for today's strip. One of Sinclair's two small strips still has a dogleg. Blakely's air strip was created from raw land but has evolved into a modern and paved strip.

Schoen sold his service in 1950, another owner ran it briefly in 1951, and by 1953, Roy Franklin became the owner of Island Sky Ferries. By taking the rear seats out of a Gull Wing Stinson he frequently provided ambulance service. Equally a part of the tapestry of the San Juans was Doctor Malcolm Heath, who was willing to board a Sky Ferries plane at any hour to patch up ailing islanders. Heath's adventures are legion, not the least of which-for Sky Ferries and Heath alike-were emergency flights in weather that ranged from bad to awful. In 1950 Heath took over the practice of a retiring San Juan Islands doctor and became a legend himself as the years went by. From a base at Friday Harbor he visited other islands as needed, first traveling by Washington State ferry, then in a relatively small boat or ISF, and eventually in an old seaplane followed by a Piper Tri-Pacer and a Cherokee 160 after he got his pilot's license.

As an example of his exploits, one time he delivered a premature baby on one of the islands and, when he determined that the baby would not live without big city hospital intervention, he put the baby in his plane. His nurse held the baby in a portable incubator while Heath's wife held an oxygen mask. Heath was met by a pediatrician in Bellingham who transferred the trio in his car to the hospital. The baby turned out fine. In 1969 Heath flew to Eastsound to minister to a couple who had crashed on takeoff in a wicked windstorm and were suffering from hypothermia and injuries. He himself landed safely, but two men had to hold down the plane after it landed until it could be parked. Undoubtedly, over the years Dr. Heath attended residents of Blakely Island. Much-respected Dr. Malcolm Heath retired in 1978 and, before he could enjoy much traveling and mountain climbing, he died.

Since most of Roy Franklin's emergency flights were for young women in labor (three in one busy night), years later a group of such island women presented Roy with an engraved plaque that read: "Honorary Stork Award presented to Roy Franklin by Mothers Making Those Unscheduled Flights."

The combination of Franklin and Heath affected Blakely on at least two occasions, not births. As described earlier, when Dal Dalles and passengers crashed at Blakely and his twin-engine plane caught on fire, the rear passengers got out safely, but Dallas and his wife were badly burned. The ambulance plane was summoned with Heath's co-worker attending. He did what he could, but a Whidbey helicopter also had been called and took the couple to Seattle's burn unit. The other incident involved my husband, Ernie Burkhart, and me as mentioned.

Ground conditions were still downright ridiculous in the 50s. One day passengers at Friday Harbor had to get out and help push their aircraft out of the mud. In 1956, ISF concluded that the company must have a modern airport at Friday Harbor, its headquarters, or quit the business. The company sold shares, mostly to local Washingtonians, at $25 each to buy the cow pasture from Lyle King and finance the building of a paved air strip, shop, hangars, and a terminal. Floyd Johnson was a major investor of 400 shares. Franklin's promise to stockholders included a vow to invest in a plane that would handle a stretcher-a Stinson Bushman-so San Juan County would have emergency medical transport. The roomy Bushman also proved to be a godsend for contracts with both Mount Baker National Forest and the Olympic National Park to drop supplies into the regions. Years later in 1970 outstanding shares from that 1950s stock sale were redeemed at $500 a share, Franklin proudly declared.

Hoping for record business from the World's Fair at Seattle of 1962, Franklin acquired a twin-engine, 10-passenger Lockheed 10 Electra. His company also had the 6-passenger Stinson Bushman and one 4-passenger Cessna 172. The company served the islands with three flights a day between Bellingham and those islands with adequate air strips. In the early 1960s the fare from Bellingham to Blakely was less than $6 and to Seattle around $11. Today a passenger from Bellingham pays more than $30, still a bargain but inflation certainly has changed the numbers.

Island Sky Ferries prospered between 1953 and 1969, after which ISF plus five other small airlines combined under the name of Puget Sound Airlines. This was a disaster for all six, and Franklin lost all his investment including airplanes before 1970 ended. Fortunately, he had not placed the airport property into the Puget Sound Airlines pot and was able to mortgage it to purchase airplanes and equipment to start over as San Juan Airlines. He operated it successfully until he sold it in 1979 and retired.

Operating out of a short air strip at Skyline right across the street from Skyline Marina, Tom Wilson operated Skyline Air Service, a charter operation that also served many Blakely residents. When the new Anacortes Airport was built, he and his successors operated from there, of course. Until 1966 all mail for Blakely and other San Juan islands went by boat, but by 1965 bidders experienced rising costs and the U.S. Postal Service found few operators willing to bid. In the fall of 1965 the Island Sky Ferries and Skyline Air Service formed a joint company called Island Mail Inc. and bid on the mail contract. Although bidders and names have changed a bit, the mail arrived reliably by air at Blakely Island for almost 40 years, and even United Parcel Service and Federal Express make deliveries to Blakely. In 2005 the mail service went full circle from 1966, serving Blakely by boat. Passenger traffic today is provided by regular and charter flights from a newer San Juan Airlines (formerly West Isle), Bellingham Aero, Island Air, and several other companies.

David Syre of Trillium Corporation. Courtesy of Trillium Corporation.

Thomas Crowley, Blakely resident and benefactor of the island.

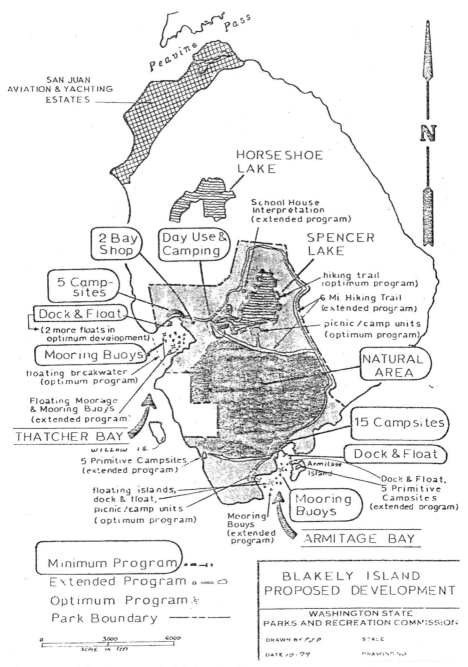

The map contains the following labels:

Peavine Pass

SAN JUAN
AVIATION & YACHTING
ESTATES

HORSESHOE
LAKE

N

School House
Interpretation
(extended program)

SPENCER
LAKE

2 Bay
Shop

Day Use &
Camping

hiking trail
(optimum program)

5 Camp-
sites

6 Mi Hiking Trail
(extended program)

Dock & Float

picnic/camp units
(optimum program)

(2 more floats in
optimum development)

Mooring Buoys

NATURAL
AREA

floating breakwater
(optimum program)

Floating Moorage
& Mooring Buoys
(extended program)

15 Campsites

THATCHER BAY

Dock & Float

WILLOW IS.

5 Primitive Campsites
(extended program)

Armitage
Island

Dock & Float,
5 Primitive
Campsites
(extended program)

floating islands,
dock & float,
picnic/camp units
(optimum program)

Mooring
Buoys

Mooring
Buoys
(extended
program)

ARMITAGE BAY

Minimum Program
Extended Program
Optimum Program
Park Boundary

BLAKELY ISLAND
PROPOSED DEVELOPMENT

WASHINGTON STATE
PARKS AND RECREATION COMMISSION

DRAWN BY PJP   SCALE

DATE 10-74   DRAWING NO

0   3000   6000
SCALE IN FEET

The proposed development of Blakely island by Washington State Parks and Recreation Commission did not go through. It would have been a drastic change of use for the island.

Chapter VII
STRIFE AND CHANGE

The legal rights of the homeowners to the use of the island were in a gray area during the initial years of the development. Early purchasers assumed that their ownership permitted their recreational use of the entire island. This was the verbal agreement. However, several adjustments to the terms of ownership had to be haggled over and clarified before these rights were sorted out legally. As a beginning, on April 4, 1970, the Blakely Island Maintenance Commission (made up of all the property owners) purchased from Floyd Johnson for $68,750 (a one-time assessment to each property owner of $360) a block of property 600 feet wide that runs across the entire island adjacent to the individual properties at the north end. This land is held as a prevention of any development there, acting as a buffer zone in the event land titles would change in future years.

Purchasers of lots at SJAYE were told verbally that they had the right to recreational use under the easement granted to the Johnsons. However, later on the homeowners were concerned about the verbal assurance, especially in the 1970s when possible developers began negotiations with Georgia-Pacific (successor to Puget Sound Pulp & Timber Company-PSPTC) for their lands. Floyd and Ola Johnson legally filed an agreement on November 10, 1973, that grants to each lot owner of SJAYE a subset of the rights they received under the easement of 1957.

Owners were startled in 1974 to learn of a plan by the State Parks and Recreation Commission for developing the tidelands of Blakely Island (see diagram in photo section) and the possible acquisition of

1260 acres from Thatcher Bay to and including Spencer Lake. Earlier Floyd Johnson and the Department of Natural Resources (DNR) concluded an agreement that quieted title of tidelands to lot owners within the platted areas and quieted the state's interest in the filled lagoon. The Parks proposal had been part of the complex negotiations at that time between Floyd Johnson (who wished to sell his Blakely interests except for a home) and prospective purchasers. The state still does own a parcel of land, some 80 acres, on the east side of the island that was originally set aside for a lighthouse.

That danger of public access through Parks or an extensive home development, however, largely disappeared in 1976 when Thomas Crowley and David Syre acquired the large upland block of 3,744 acres. The agony of threshing out that achievement is a complex saga. I am indebted to my friend and famous writer Archie Satterfield for some of the information about this turbulent period. Satterfield wrote a company history of Trillium that included some details pertinent to Blakely. David Syre and a representative for the Crowley family added material. Here's the way it went:

Well-known Northwest developer David Syre of the Trillium Corporation was a principal in the saga. In the 1960s Syre was a local farm boy who had become a lawyer. He preferred to use his knowledge for property development projects with one of his earliest involvements being the fate of Blakely Island. Syre become involved with Blakely through a Seattle developer, Gil Johnston, a one-time teacher at the correctional institute on Cypress Island. Johnston had a grand vision of creating an Islands of the World complex that would work something like a time-share operation. An owner would be able to use condos or facilities on islands all over the world. He tapped Blakely to be the San Juan Islands island paradise for the group and asked Bellingham attorney David Syre to arrange an option with Georgia-Pacific for purchase of their holdings, 3,744 of the 4,300 acres.

As Johnston's lawyer Syre was drawn into the Islands plan and started negotiations with Georgia-Pacific (GP) to facilitate the proposed Islands of the World development, he discovered a maze of problems. Among them, Floyd had reserved most of the island's shoreline about 600 feet back for possible future development. At the time of initial contacts with Johnson (1973) the easement rights of lot owners to use the upper island for recreational purposes still had to be formalized, too, as mentioned above. Blakely's homeowners were incensed and worried about the future of the island and, as Syre himself commented, he then was 34 years old, had long hair and a beard, and did not foster the islanders' confidence in doing right by them.

When time came to put up the option money in 1973, Gil Johnston suggested that Syre go fifty-fifty with him.. Syre alone made the initial option payment of $60,000. The total purchase price was to be $1.9 million to GP and more than $600,000 to Floyd Johnson for those lands from Armitage-Homestead and Thatcher Bay that he had retained under the initial sale to PSPTC. The large sum appeared feasible by the potential value of the marketable timber on the island. Syre then was not a large financier as he is today and had to borrow just the option money from the bank. He could not possibly come up with the purchase price but received an eight-months extension from GP to see what he could do. The Blakely Island homeowners were up in arms, reacting to rumors of high-rise condos to be built along the marina's shore, five-acre lots to be platted across the entire island, rampant timber harvesting, ferry stops, and such. However, the Commission and its members had meager legal recourse because they did not own the G-P lands, of course.

To say that homeowners were very agitated about the future of their island paradise would be a gross understatement. According to June 1974 board minutes it was rumored that Sun-Mark Property Development of Bellingham (under an agreement involving David Syre) planned to develop 500 acres of Blakely property into 2,000 to 3,000 condominiums at a location not mentioned there, plus develop 200 five-acre lots adjacent to the buffer strip. The period from 1973 to 1975-76 when Tom Crowley stepped up to solve the concerns of the islanders was very turbulent and fraught with rumor mills, outrage, frustration, and indecision. However, since most worries were resolved, it is futile to review the situation more than briefly.

To add to the dilemmas facing both Syre and the homeowners, a strong movement developed with pages of news coverage in the Northwest to make all of the San Juan Islands an international park. Gil Johnston still had some sort of ownership rights in the development agreement hc had signed with Syre, and sold his rights (half) to a Tacoma group called Talmo, made up of Jim Tallman and Thomas Morris. This company was particularly interested in the timber on the island. Rumors of clear cutting did not ease Blakely homeowners' worries, although Syre said that would not be a good idea if the direction for development would be second home use.

The entire future of the upper island was in limbo for both Syre and the homeowners. Financial matters for Syre needed attention. Attorneys among Blakely's homeowners threatened to file suits against him. William H. Carlson of Orcas Island filed suit against Syre, claiming Syre had promised him, David MacBryer, and Thomas Morris the logging contract on Blakely. The suit was settled out of court. Syre had become associated with Sun-Mark Company, developers of Sudden Valley outside Bellingham. Syre tried to work his way out of the investment he had made, largely indebtedness he personally had incurred for the $2.6 million price he paid to G-P and Johnson for the inner island lands. He attended the Blakely homeowner meetings as often as possible, meetings obviously hostile since portions of homeowners' recreational use were threatened. To Syre's credit (and certainly he was not the most popular person on Blakely at the time), he did try to ameliorate what concerns he could and not change the whole character of the islands, while trying to proceed with his development plans. As indicated above, he had $2.6 million hanging out there.

In June 1975 he drew up a questionnaire and sent it to all Blakely landowners. Here is the text:

Our first land-use plan for the approximate 3,800 acres on Blakely Island was to establish dense condominium development in the Spencer and Thatcher Bay areas [not near the marina as the rumor had been], while leaving the remainder of the island, with the exception of a few large tracts, in greenbelt. This plan was not favorable to Blakely Island Maintenance Commission members and failed due to financial problems confronted by Sun-Mark Development and their real estate investment trust principal, Continental Mortgage investors. Thereafter, we spent several months with the Washington State Parks Commission and Nature conservancy, complying with their wishes to purchase some 1,260 acres in the Thatcher Bay, Armitage Bay and Spencer Lake areas.

Their proposal to purchase unanimously supported by the Washington State Parks Commission, the interagency council for recreation in the State of Washington, and then upon reaching legislature, failed due to political disagreements between the legislative process and State Parks. Though State Parks still has a very sincere interest in establishing a park on Blakely Island, the possibility of the same becoming a reality is quite remote. Before starting any additional planning of Blakely Island, we wish to have the comments and suggestions of individual lot owners as to their interest in additional buffer zone and/or privately owned acreage and what they would wish to see as development on the island and in what areas they would wish the same to be completed.

On purchases of property, the prices and terms are negotiable.

1. Would you wish to be part of a limited partnership organized to purchase additional buffer areas including Horseshoe Lake? If so, how many acres?
2. Would you wish the Blakely Island Maintenance Commission to purchase additional buffer zones? If yes, how many acres?
3. Would you be interested in purchase of acres to hold in individual ownership? If yes, how many acres? Where?
4. Would you be interested, as members of the Maintenance Commission, to have that commission enter into a joint agreement with Syre-Talmo for the management of Horseshoe Lake?
5. What would you wish to see in terms of planning on Blakely Island?

Understandably the homeowners were distressed and vocal but, once again, the facts were clear. Originally, Floyd Johnson had sold those inner lands to Puget Sound Pulp & Timber, who sold them to Georgia-Pacific, and now were optioned for purchase by David Syre or Syre-Talmo. As he was one of the regular homeowners, Tom Crowley received the questionnaire and called David Syre. Syre said later that he had no idea who Crowley was until he talked with Don Fitzpatrick. Fitz told him that, if Crowley wanted to talk with him, he had better see what he wanted. Of course, not then known to Syre, Crowley was the descendant of the famed San Francisco Crowley maritime family that dated back to 1892. The company was the largest privately held tug and barge (plus ships and other vessels) firm in the world and highly regarded for its integrity. Indeed, Crowley barges rescued San Franciscans from the 1906 fire by moving out onto San Francisco Bay with hundreds aboard.

In his usual unassuming, low-key fashion Tom said he didn't know anything about real estate and offered Syre $100,000 for all the lands north of Spencer. Of course, this was not enough, because that portion alone was worth $1 million at the time. Syre believed that Tom was not really interested, yet was puzzled because he continued to contact him off and on. During this time Blakely homeowner Doug Moreton was very instrumental in pressuring both Floyd Johnson and Tom Crowley to cooperate with Syre in working out some kind of agreement acceptable to all. Syre credits Moreton as the matchmaker between himself and Crowley. However, by summer's end the potential partnership was deadlocked. Syre told Crowley he was going to go ahead, because he did not believe Crowley was really interested. Tom said he was but did not do anything. Syre placed a portion of the lands for sale with Chris Turlis, a realtor. Turlis contacted Crowley, who purportedly almost jumped over the table as to why Syre hadn't told him he was going to do that. The negotiations thereafter became serious.

Crowley, Pete Taggares, and John Leslie (the latter two being Blakely homeowners) offered to buy a strip of land across the island adjacent to the buffer zone. The offer was fair but did not materialize. Instead, Tom Crowley asked to become Syre's partner in the Blakely Island holdings, to which David Syre agreed. The two particularly were disturbed at the extent of Talmo's logging of the island and wanted this stopped. Crowley bought out Talmo for $250,000 cash. The loggers who had been hired by Talmo were miffed at the sudden loss of their potential logs and allegedly came in the night to haul off more rafts of logs. This practice was soon discovered and stopped.

Now that Syre and Crowley were partners, they made plans to take control of the island, to stop the logging, and manage their properties. They opened negotiations with Floyd Johnson to buy out the remaining 8-10 years of the marina operator's lease and about 70 undeveloped lots. The lots would give them the clout they desired in voting on

Blakely Island Maintenance Commission matters. Ola Johnson and an aging Floyd were growing weary of trying to control the direction of island development. Syre claimed that, by now, with all the time he had spent on the island and in negotiations that involved Floyd at times, he and Floyd were almost like father and son in a good and friendly relationship. The result was that Floyd sold the marina and lots to the Syre-Crowley partnership for $80,000. That hurdle cleared, they worked on plans for lower density residential development to preserve the naturalness of the island.

From 1974 to 1976, Syre and Crowley worked toward a conservation easement of some sort to create a tax savings that would chiefly be assigned to Crowley. The tax savings could help to recover his advancements of capital to the partnership. They hired the Nature Conservancy personnel to do an environmental inventory. The results disclosed that they owned about 800 acres of old growth never cut on the east shore and some grass ridges on the south end that were important because similar ridges no longer existed on the other San Juan Islands. Rare bat colonies and eagle habitat existed. An attorney wrote a conservation easement proposal, allegedly the first conservation easement in Washington State..

The duo planned to give the property to the Nature Conservancy, but the latter required a maximum of five new homes, none visible from the water, whereas the partnership hoped for 60 homes with salt water views eventually. As the deadline of December 31, 1976, rapidly approached, Syre and Crowley had yet to decide the recipient of the proposed gift. Because one of the lawyers, "Skeeter" Ellis, working on the proposal had attended Seattle Pacific University, the donors approached them. You can imagine how startled the staff was. Here was a multi-million dollar gift of 910 acres of land being offered, with the only provision that SPU provide a scientific research center. Furthermore, Crowley offered to cover the shortfall of expenses over tuition of SPU for a limited time. A conservation easement was drawn up for 2,334 acres, said to be the first such easement in Washington (the easement did allow Crowley 30 sites for future development) . The donation was accepted before the deadline as a fee-simple ownership and conservation easement, and Crowley received substantial tax relief. Syre received development land of 500 acres at the south end. (All this totals 3,744 upland acres originally purchased.) The partnership put the marina and undeveloped lots it had purchased into another corporation. After the property division was complete, Syre and Crowley dissolved their partnership.

As complex and heated as the long land negotiations were, most of the players received, if not all, at least most of what each wanted. The massive housing development so feared by northenders did not occur and cannot under the present easements. Syre was able to recover his investment and, having fallen under Blakely's spell himself, was content that the massive development plan had not occurred, after all. SPU was a massive beneficiary of unforeseen donations.

Tom Crowley's gift of shoring up the shortfall of expenses over tuition for SPU continued until 1993, when he established an endowment fund of $2 million for SPU's Blakely Campus, instead. David Syre and his firm Trillium Corporation contributed $200,000 to this same fund.

Crowley also realized that the 910 acres of SPU land carried no prohibitions against development. He negotiated an agreement with SPU that exchanged certain Blakely Island lands needed by SPU for other lands owned by SPU, and placed a restriction on all of SPU's Blakely lands against any residential development. This provision assured that the SPU land would be used only for educational purposes.

The 1976 agreement had given Crowley 30 permissible residential sites. He sold one to Doug Moreton. In December 1993 he gave the San Juan Preservation Trust (SJPT) a conservation easement reducing the permissible sites to 19. Two days before his death on July 7, 1994, he executed a third easement reducing the number of permissible sites to only four and mailed it to his agent in San Juan County. It was not delivered to SJPT until after Tom's death, and attorneys for the estate advised that the gift was not completed. Thus, the number of sites remains at 19. No residential development except for the home of Doug Moreton (now the residence of BC and Christine Crowley) has occurred.

Tom Crowley, who was one of the most unassuming yet influential persons on Blakely Island, certainly endeared himself to the homeowners for helping to save the character of the island. Typically he was very modest about his significant donation to SPU, saying to a reporter who asked him about it, that he had a little summer place up there at Blakely and wanted to keep it peaceful...or something like that. He died in 1994 at age 79, and his ashes are contained in a memorial granite bench at the lower end of Blakely Summit's cleared area

An additional sifting out of ownerships of Blakely Island occurred during the late 1970s, when Pete Taggares decided to buy Syre's half interest in the marina and the surrounding grassy area toward Driftwood Beach (the former marsh), entering into a partnership with Tom Crowley for its operation as the Blakely Island Company, Syre and Crowley's 1976 organization.

Now that Syre owned the south end property he and an architect from Bellingham looked over the waterfront, decided on 30 good home sites, mostly five acres each, to be sold and the rest was placed in a green belt designation. The corporation resulting from this decision, Armitage Blakely, Inc., in 1979 sold 295 acres to South Bay Associates (SBA), essentially a group of 16 people who sought to build residential homes at the south end. The area was platted into 20 lots, each fronting on the ocean and ranging from 5 to 17 acres per lot. The area behind the lots was declared a common area. The residents manage their own utilities and hired a caretaker to live in a cabin near the dock at the south end built by Steve Kennedy. Chet and Mabel Brandt were the first SBA caretakers, followed by Lyle/Linda Litch, Kass and Dean Mazur, Pete/Robin Lamont, Cliff/Marti Curtiss, and Norma/Rick Reed at this writing.

The few SBA residents live individual lives by choice, for the most part, unlike the teeming activities of the San Juan Aviation Estates. One of the few notable incidents, one most regrettable, was that in 2004 the lovely home of Doug and Nancy Norberg at Homestead Bay caught fire and was destroyed totally, despite the concerted efforts of volunteer fire crews from BIMC and SBA. The fire was caused by rodents damaging wiring in the heating system! In 2005, a beach fire got away from participants near Homestead and into the brush but was quickly controlled.

The first Seattle Pacific university building, built by G. Plume.

Dr. Ross Shaw.
The first manager of SPU Blakely Campus.

Dedication of SPU Blakely Campus. Sen. Slade Gordon holds the right side of ribbon.

Chapter VIII
UNIVERSITY CAMPUS AND MARINAS

Remembered only by a few long-time residents present in the 1960s a forest fire threatened briefly very near to today's SPU campus location. Lightning struck a tree beside the main south road, corkscrewing down the trunk and igniting some underbrush. Residents galvanized into action with shovels and extinguishers and headed up island, while others took off in planes to pinpoint the location of the fire. The underbrush smoldered but did not catch fire seriously. A small sign identified the "Lightning Tree" for many years. It was created by Phyllis Galbraith and Lance Douglas, then a little boy, who were walking near the tree the day after it was hit.

After the donation to SPU of the upper island lands in 1976, little occurred there until December 1975, when Gordon Plume designed the first and very imaginative building for SPU. Plume was Tom Crowley's previous brother-in-law; his first wife Susie and Tom's wife Fifi were sisters. Trained in stone masonry and wood working, Gordon built an unusual stone path up to Taggares's "cookshack" or conference building, renovated several old cabins at the plat, and completed some small projects for SBA and SPU. He also constructed the new Spencer bathtub (the original had been stolen by an off-island person) at Tom Crowley's request. He had acquired a reputation as a creative wood worker; thus, when the time came for SPU to raise its first building, he was selected to do the design.

The walls of the hexagonal building used as a dining room, laboratory, and meeting room are constructed of wood blocks stacked and reinforced within in a manner similar to the way concrete blocks in mortar would be used-called cordwood masonry . Plume had to gain approval from the Architectural Review Board before building the structure. He said, "The architect there said 'you want to do WHAT? why not just build a log building?' and thought it would not work." SPU believed in Gordon's work and supported his idea. The board approved the design, and the walls have weathered to a pleasant gray tone. An additional conversation piece for the building is the lovely ceiling of the library. It radiates out into a circle from a central focal point and is made from 2x4s shaped to fit, nailed, finished and certainly innovative. It is supported by an upside down stump. That building and others complete the present SPU campus.

Gordon and his crew built several of the South Bay Associates homes, including Runstad and Stansbury. Steve Kennedy of Orcas Island built the caretaker's home at Armitage and Norberg's log cabin that burned in 2004. Plume's work on the SPU buildings earned him an invitation to design portions of Microsoft's Bill Gates' home. For the past two decades the Plumes have lived and operated a specialized wood design factory at Bellingham, where they live in a modern home. It is quite different from the rigors of the remote rural life Gordon and his bride Robin lived at Thatcher Bay between 1975 and 1985.

The Plumes had no electricity for light or heat their first winter of 1975. For heating and cooking they had a wood stove in the kitchen and in the living room. For baths in the old claw foot tub they heated water on the stove, pioneer style. Water came from a gravity feed system from Spencer Lake. The Plumes' only communication with the outside world was a telephone in one of the old cabins at the north end of the SJAYE airstrip. Robin drove there from Thatcher and sat in an unheated cabin to do construction ordering and scheduling, later with her baby son Eric in a snuggly. The Plumes enthusiastically worked with OPALCO while they were building the sub-station to hasten receipt of electricity at Thatcher and, when they finally got a telephone at Thatcher, Robin danced for joy.

Eric and Virginia Plume were born five years apart while the Plumes lived in rural splendor at Thatcher, probably the first babies born on Blakely Island since the homesteaders. Each time Gordon flew Robin off the island to a hospital while she was in labor. Robin says that in the summer of 1984, there was a posting of a survey pool for islanders visiting Spencer Lake: "Should Gordon and Robin have a second baby?" The whimsy was attributed to Anne Malmo. Many votes were received, and Virginia was born the following summer. Later Robin went for walks with the baby in a large blue carriage with the largest wheels she could find, because all-terrain carriages were not yet made. The children's playmates as toddlers were the cats, dog, and chickens, including an ornery rooster that tried to spur Robin and met his demise shortly thereafter for his pains. The rooster's replacement was gentle and kind but would not sleep in the henhouse; it preferred to roost in the trees. Raccoons were a constant threat to the chickens.

When Eric became of school age, he first was flown to the Orcas school on the mail plane, like the Tompkins and White children were. The pilots called him "pip-squeak," and it was a long day for a little boy. In second grade he attended the last remote-by-necessity schoolhouse in Washington on Decatur Island. He was the only child there not related to the other students. Every morning he was dropped off by boat at a remote dock and walked a quarter mile through the woods to the schoolhouse. One foggy mid-September morning he couldn't find the school so returned to the beach. There a teacher returning from a work day at Lopez found him in the afternoon, still waiting for someone to come.

While he was working at Blakely, Plume was made a special deputy sheriff for San Juan County for a time. This required little except making sure unauthorized persons did not land on the SBA and SPU property and gain access to the island. However, on one occasion, he found a canoe on the south end tied to a tree that bore a sign "No Trespassing." He untied the canoe, left a note for the unknown trespasser, and took the canoe home. A few days later the sheriff at Friday Harbor called to say a man reported that someone stole his canoe on Blakely. Eventually the matter was straightened out

For a time the Plumes kept two cows for beef. They ran wild but one day wandered down to SJAYE. This would never do, as they might damage airplanes or be on the runway. Cal Courtright (115), a veteran cattle rancher, helped to lasso the pair and drag them back to the south end. After he captured each cow, he dramatically threw his arms up and out like a rodeo cowboy. The men carried the tied-up critters in a backhoe back to Thatcher!

When the cows returned a third time, Phyllis Tucker tried to help and lassoed one of the animals, using a rope that had a large pulley block attached to one end. She could not hold the cow, and it ran off with the metal pulley clanking along. Fearing damage to planes or property. With some help Gordon managed to corral the cows, but not before one knocked him down and walked on him. He summoned a butcher to shoot the two and take their carcasses to Lopez to become hamburger. The most bizarre aspect to this tale is that the Plumes discovered the meat saw and grinders used were allegedly the same rumored (but never proved) to be used by a convicted murderess to dispatch her husband. The Plumes were unable to stomach the concept of eating the beef and gave it away.

The Plumes' next adventure with wild animals was gentler. One day an unusually tame, apparently orphaned fawn came to their Thatcher house. Robin adopted it. It hung out at the Spencer Lake orchard for some time, where islanders came to pet it and feed it goodies, but it became a pest for the Plumes. The fawn wanted to come into the house and actually jumped over a Dutch door to get inside. Having a tame fawn around no longer was fun, and Robin gave it to Rose Anne Raymond at the settlement. It was no small feat to get it into a pickup and haul the struggling animal down there; but Roseanne fell in love with the fawn. Roseanne even let is sleep on her davenport. It followed her everywhere. Unfortunately, later on it died of unknown causes. Meantime, one day a pair of teens came from the bay to Plumes' home to ask if they had seen a fawn. As the conversation progressed, the teens confessed that the fawn had been their pet in Sudden Valley, Bellingham, and that the Game Department wanted to confiscate it, so they put it in a boat and turned it loose on Blakely.

While Plume was building parts of the campus, in 1976 SPU assigned Don Kurlee the over-all responsibility for its Blakely campus and Dr. Ross Shaw the on-site management. In the summer of 1977 SPU used a surveyor to look at the lands donated to them and by easement and to suggest management plans for use of the site in teaching programs. The first class was held in summer 1978 at the bathtub house (Spencer cabin). Twelve students of teen or preteen age and Dr. Shaw himself spent a week living at the cabin and experiencing pioneer life. A new well near the creek supplied good water. An old outhouse was temporarily usable until a better one could be built. Shaw and helpers located a second-hand, propane, apartment-size stove of four burners and an oven for cooking. They placed an ice chest in the stream. Girls occupied one upstairs bedroom, boys the other, and Shaw the main floor bedroom. A tent in back of the cabin provided additional quarters. Shaw's wife did not join him at Blakely until 1982, after some campus buildings were completed. Shaw said that their first invitation to dinner at the settlement came from Don and Cheryl Burkhart.

Basic educational agendas were laid out. Shaw said, "We held classes until about four each day, then repaired to Horseshoe Lake to swim. That first year we worked with Gordon Plume milling lumber with a saw, and the lumber was later used in the campus building. At night when I was about to go to sleep, I actually could hear carpenter ants working on the cabin. Lance Douglas helped us get rid of them."

After some maintenance to the bathtub house in the early 1980s, SPU began holding special classes for its summer students or for children's writing classes at the cabin. Some Blakely children attended. Considering its remote location, the children surely must have felt like pioneers after sleeping and eating there. Some reported it spooky and wondered if ghosts dwelled there. Others reveled in the primitive life. In 1981, Tamara Katz wrote:

> I slept in the cabin that was small,
> I went to school in a little cottage,
> I saw the hornbook. It was neat.
> We got to read from an old book.
> We did relay races and Josie and I tied.
> I like it when we had a spelling test.
> We went on hikes almost every day.
> I liked it when we washed clothes.

Another wrote, "Sometimes I wish I was a pioneer. You'd get to wash by hand, sew, grind wheat, milk cows...and you'd have to cut grass for the animals."

One of the most unusual groups to come for a Spencer cabin class was from a Seattle Hebrew school that scheduled with SPU for the summer program. A rabbi came to make everything kosher. The children were from fifth to eighth grade. Shaw said, "We had a goat and built a milking platform so the kids learned to milk it and make cheese. We also made soap from lye and tallow." The visit came about because Ivy Kurlee (wife of Don) taught at the Hebrew school. She also taught a summer class at SPU Blakely.

Another summer SPU staff discovered two goats that had been abandoned on Blakely-no connection with the milking goat. The goats hung around and were quite aggressive, chasing the children.

Later Shaw told me, "The director of our facility at Camp Casey, Whidbey Island, came one day and was hunting. He ran across the goats and shot them for us. He also got a deer and took all three carcasses to Oak Harbor for processing. Well, the butcher was suspicious about why we had the three and called the game warden. After we explained the situation, we did not get arrested."

While the SPU campus dominated news at the south end of Blakely Island, the Blakely Marina was the center of action at SJYAE. Following the demise of colorful Bayliss Harriss, families named Dale, Washibaugh and Osborn operated the marina until 1978. Most subsequent operators have lived in the second floor marina apartment. They included Bob and Robyn Raftery 1980, Jim and Gayle Parish 1981-? Norma and Lloyd Garceau 1986-? Chuck and Pam Reed for one year, Lloyd and Deneane Thurman from 1991-95, assisted from 1993-95 by Mary and Bob Farmer because DeNeane was then pregnant. The Thurmans chose to live at the Thatcher Bay caretaker's house and the Farmers above the marina. The Farmers remained on the island several years after their marina duties, performing various other caretaking positions. During Barbara (Mrs. Ross) Shaw's session with cancer, they assisted in management of the SPU campus. Barbara and Duffy Nightingale were the marina operators from 1995-97, followed by Robin and Peter Lamont 1997-99, and Norma and Rick Reed from February 1999 to the present writing. Dozens of Blakely's teenagers have benefited from summer jobs cashiering or helping in maintenance of the marina and gas docks.

Life as a marina manager or facilities manager can be routine or punctuated by moments of sheer drama. Such was the case on April 14, 2002, when Norma Reed called Jim Davis for help in rescuing a sailboat in trouble at the gas dock. A severe wind buffeted the 32-foot boat with waves running five to six feet. They threatened to roll the boat over onto the dock or else rip the dock loose. Owners were hypothermic, and waves rolling over the gas dock soaked to their waists everyone that tried to assist them. When attempts to walk the craft around the dock to the inside failed, Jim jumped aboard. When Davis's attempts to run the boat around to the inside also failed, he decided to make for the turbulent marina entrance. In pitch dark and working only from instinct and memory, he and the owners were able to get the craft safely into the marina. Norma Reed collected the owners and wrapped them in blankets at the marina apartment.

Weather brings refugees into the marina, many of them boaters that dare not risk crossing Rosario Strait in high seas or fog. The Strait is the main shipping channel between Seattle and Vancouver and for ocean-going ships entering Puget Sound from the Strait of Juan de Fuca. Such large vessels, some of them oil tankers or freighters, create huge wakes that can swamp small boats that venture too close. The long reach of Rosario Strait can sustain large swells and choppy wind waves. Other yachtsmen limp into Blakely with boat trouble. On one fall day a charter boat came in for gas during a power outage. Without power one cannot pump gas. A passenger aboard had to get to the mainland and catch a plane for an important meeting. After several hours without power and with a fretting visitor, the Reeds went looking for the fuel truck and siphoned off enough to get the charter boat to Anacortes. Another boat owner and wife took refuge at the marina with engine trouble. Rick Reed took them to Anacortes to arrange for a new manifold and other parts, then returned them to Blakely to await delivery. Four days later they were under way. The people said they enjoyed their stay and have returned frequently with their friends.

Still another family came into the marina with an ailing boat and left on the passenger boat *Paraclete* to Anacortes. They did not return at all, apparently planning to abandon the boat. Marina personnel called the sheriff and then the Lummi Tribal Government (at his suggestion) and gained permission to put the boat out of the marina on a buoy. The father of the boat owner finally managed to get it towed back to the reservation and thanked the marina owners warmly for their trouble.

Today the marina's policy for transient boaters in trouble is that they must stay on the island with their boat until it is fixed, paid for, and removed, and not leave the island. Of course, Blakely owners are not required to do so. During the Reeds' first year on the job homeowners Dan Roach and Ellen Roth left the marina in their older wooden boat, then returned but went off island by air. Within a few hours employees noticed that the boat had sunk with only the bow sticking out of the water. Somehow they dragged the boat over to the ramp and got a trailer under it, with Terry Pence and the Reeds intermittently wading in the water.

The marina operators regularly find themselves trying to straighten out people's problems. One night a guest from a boat had hiked up into the buffer strip. Darkness fell and, when he had not returned, the marina personnel instituted a search. The man had become lost in the deep forest but was located by midnight. On their second day as marina operators the Reeds had to minister to an injured boater. After refusing help from personnel in docking their boat on a very windy day, the couple got into the marina all right but, when the husband jumped off the bow of the boat, he caught his foot on the rail and landed on a cleat, injuring his knee. He was able to get around after some assistance but confessed that he was supposed to start a new job that very next day and now would not make it.

Even routine tasks are challenging. Groceries and supplies arrive at Obstruction Pass dock by truck, and the marina packet must meet that truck, no matter what the weather. Norma Reed said that going over to Obstruction in a dense fog can be pretty interesting. Power outages are a nightmare. One occurred for six hours a few years ago, and they had to move all their frozen foods into emergency space.

Racoons entertained and aggravated Blakely homeowners.

The Baird sisters enjoyed the empty Blakely trails.

The marina in 2002. Photo by Robert Foote.

Every vehicle and large supply item came by packet from Obstruction Pass.

A wonderful view from the marina road toward Eastbound.

Chapter IX
INCIDENTS, ACCIDENTS & PEOPLE

Maritime and aviation accidents do happen. Don Spawn, who built his home on Signal Beach (Rogich now), anchored his boat on a buoy. Jim Fergus says that, while Spawn was away in the late 70s, his boat was discovered sunk to the gunwales and drifting ashore. While Charlie and Margaret Mills and Del Smith tried to hold it off the beach and prevent it from grounding fast, Jim got a boat and came to the rescue. He towed Spawn's boat into the marina while Charlie Mills, soaking wet, rode in the swamped boat. The volunteers pumped it out, and no serious damage had occurred, although Jim said, "There was water in every locker we opened."

A riveting diversion one 1980s afternoon during one of the infamous Eastsound winds injured an airplane but not the owner. A visitor in a Beech Bonanza attempted to land north to south, was way too high, and aborted the landing. He pulled up his gear, went around, returned and aborted a second time. He pulled up the gear again, went around but this time he forgot to lower the gear, landed with a crunch, and put on power as his prop disintegrated. This caused him to shoot off the south end of the runway to wind up nose down in the water. Seeing all this happening, Don Burkhart leaped on his cycle, speeded down to the south end, and dove into the water to save the man. When he got to the plane, he found a nearby resident had a boat in the water, the pilot got out by himself, and all was well. Every one returned to the beach, wet but alive. The unidentified visitor was a very chagrined airline pilot, so embarrassed that he barely would talk to anyone on the island. His airplane was last seen on a trailer leaving the island behind a truck.

In the mid-1960s caretaker Scott McCulloch's father landed in a Cessna new to him, wiped out the nose wheel, and skidded down the runway in flames. Jack McCulloch jumped out of the moving plane and rolled, surviving without injury, before the plane exploded and burned totally.

While most Blakelyites arrive by air or boat, others arrive by car at Obstruction Pass, then seek transportation of themselves and goods, often a car or large piece of furniture, across the water to Blakely. Because Blakely residents did not use the county's allotted road money, in 1991 San Juan County built a dock at Obstruction Pass for the use of Blakely residents (and others, too). At first the county found it difficult to find available shore property on which to build, but they succeeded. The Blakely Marina is a big user of the dock to facilitate the receipt of grocery shipments. Today the marina has its own small ferry for this purpose.

The only business other than the marina and home construction was real estate. In 1978, a businessman and his wife from Seattle, Jim and Judy Tompkins, came to live full-time at Blakely, along with their two school-age children. Jim spent weekdays at Kirkland and weekends on Blakely, so his arriving plane on Friday night or Saturday became a familiar sight For a time Judy was chiefly a housewife and mom, but later went to work for Floyd Johnson's real estate office. Living year-round at Blakely opens different challenges from vacation life. Like the earlier school children from Blakely Glen and Brin, ages nine and ten at that time, were taken to Obstruction Pass dock by boat to catch the school bus. When they were older, they ran the boat over themselves. During high school for two years San Juan Airlines took them to Eastsound . When the airline required the boys to fit into their existing schedules, which meant arriving late and leaving school early each day, the Tompkins decided to return to boat transportation. The boys were interviewed for an article by a reporter for USA Today. While Paul and Anne Malmo lived on Blakely for a time, their two daughters-Catherine and Elizabeth-attended Orcas Schools. Chuck White's son Chandler also attended Orcas schools in 1979 and 1980, graduating in 1980.

For a time the Tompkins enjoyed a cute pet, an orphaned raccoon they bottle-fed and named Rax. As he grew, Judy said, "He was a combination of a cat and dog. He would curl up in your lap like a cat but play tug of war like a dog. If we needed to catch him and he ran off like it was a game, we lured him to the tennis court, where we could catch him easier." He would walk along the top of the net easily. One day Judy and Jim were trying to pick crab, but Rax was persistently trying to get into their yard and eat it. When they put him in the tennis court, he was older now and could climb the fence. He was back at the house as quickly as they were.

Rac wandered around, although not too far from the Tompkins house, then located at the south end of the airstrip. One day he went to dinner with the family at Don Spawn's house at the beach and some- how a clam closed shut on one paw. A heated tool and a hot poker on its shell failed to make it release. Tired out from his frenzied efforts to get rid of the clam, Rax went upstairs and went to sleep, clam and all. "We had to get it off his finger-like paw or it might cut off circulation," said Judy. "While we were trying to catch him, since he was frantic when you even touched him, he accidentally got his paw caught in the fire extinguisher bracket, pulled on it, and the shell popped off." He licked and licked the creases in his fingers, and they recovered.

Sadly they found Rax shot dead on the beach. Perhaps someone pur- posely did the deed, because he was getting into other people's houses, but the Tompkins also felt he might have been shot accidentally, mistak- en for a second raccoon around the area that was aggressive and mean.

Wally Weller, another year-round resident, tangled with the wildlife, too. Tired of hearing raccoons walking around on his roof, he climbed up and literally kicked them off. Wally's verdant garden attracts hopeful deer, one of which got its head under the garden gate, panicked, raised up and lifted the gate off the hinges. It was tangled up in the gate, got loose, and after a merry chase around the premises, finally was shooed out without getting into the airplane hangar and doing damage. In the past, Don Fitzpatrick Sr. hit a deer on landing and sustained no damage, except to the deer, but Jerry Pringle was not as lucky and damaged his plane in a similar accident.

During a windstorm in 1989 the power was off for 12 hours. Trees went down on the power lines and were tangled together on the ground, so Judy Tompkins did not dare to walk near them. The Mills walked down the beach to see if Judy was all right, avoiding the downed tree/power line messes on the road. Meanwhile, Jim Tompkins was unsuccessfully trying to reach Judy or anyone on Blakely, and failing, actually flew in when the wind abated only slightly. Some lovely cedars that Pete Raymond had planted at Driftwood and carefully irrigated were wrecked, as well. At Lummi Island the northeast wind was clocked at 100 mph. OPALCO put out a booklet on this, a 100-year storm, but in 1990 an equally bad wind arose. The DNR (Department of Natural Resources) estimated that six million board feet of timber was down on Blakely alone. Judy was destined to survive a later big storms alone, too, because, in 1996, Jim had just left the island before the incredibly huge snow storm occurred, described later.

In 1980 Anne and Paul Malmo lived full-time on the island while they made plans for a new business. Judy and Ann recall watching the drama of getting Dan O'Brien's house onto its Driftwood Beach site. The home was in two sections on a landing craft, too wide, it ensued, to get into the marina. The Driftwood Beach gravel "gives," and the crew had to take off part of the landing craft to get enough height to unload the two sections. They unloaded one section and, as it was headed up the slope, the tow mechanism on the truck started to fail. Frantic crew members grabbed firewood to put under the wheels when the load actually began to go backwards. Further troubles were that a big windstorm had downed trees on the sides of the road, which rubbed against the sections and removed some of the facie. When the two halves of the house were in place, the crew discovered that they had unloaded the wrong section first and the part that was to face the water....didn't. All was straightened out eventually.

Floyd Johnson lost his beloved partner and wife Ola in 1980. A bench at the marina is dedicated to her memory. As much as Floyd, she surely was a key person in the development of Blakely Island, as she lived at the SJAYE plat to manage the promotional matters and on-site property sales full time in the early years, while Floyd was gone. The year 1980 was further marred for Floyd by an injury to his back that left him unable to engage in many aspects of managing Blakely's future. A year or so later, however, he remarried Joan, whose sister Kay Weiland Alley was a resident of Blakely for many years.

122

A fixture for Blakely-ites has been the arrival of the Christmas ship each year about two or three weeks before Christmas Day. Currently the Lions Club of Bellingham sponsors the ship, which arrives with volunteer crews to distribute small gifts, caroling, and good cheer to several of the San Juan Islands not served by ferry. Some Blakely families fly in with their children (or no children) to meet the ship as part of their holiday traditions. Usually the weather is wild and woolly in December, and ship crews often have memorable trips through the outer channels of the islands, offset by the happy faces of those who greet them at isolated ports.

Blakely's Fourth of July celebrations have become bigger. A tradition of holding a potluck gathering on the holiday for all islanders began as early as 1980. In fact, in 1982, the party was a street dance at the marina with boaters invited, too. No one fell into the bay, and everyone agreed it was enjoyable. Another year or two the picnic was held on Driftwood Beach. Eventually the event moved to the marina picnic shelter. In 2005 the gathering again included live music and dancing.

The Fourth was and is a noisy time. Some time ago on a wet Fourth not threatened by fire danger teenagers mounted a barrel on the back of a jeep and set off fire crackers inside it, creating deafening explosions, while they drove around the plat's roads. With the exception of one year when all fireworks were banned due to drought and fire danger islanders gathered along the beach facing Peavine Pass to set off fireworks over the bay. In later years the Obstruction Islanders shot their fireworks over the water toward Blakely in mock battles. Parents kept reasonable safety rules, and no one was hurt-with the exception of a small burn here and there. In 2003 Scott and Lisa Burkhart initiated a Fourth of July parade. They invited all children to the Burkhart lawn and handed out paper decorations or encouraged them to bring their own to decorate bikes, motorcycles, cars, and even riding lawn mowers. The event grows each year.

Some past members of the Blakely family were memorable. .The advent of Pete Taggares to the island's residential rolls afforded some interest. Island children remember him as giving Jack Bartram a $100 tip for picking him up one day at the air strip and driving him to his home. As Bartram's friend said, "resulting in the kids road-rally reaction later to be the first to greet him when his plane landed." After his purchase of the peninsula across from the marina, and adjacent grassland, Pete had the Bartram construction team build a fine home and building called the "cook shack" on his property, where he could entertain and confer with clients and friends. Taggares's hobby was operating heavy equipment, so he brought a mower and other equipment over to Blakely to enjoy. He painted everything he owned white, including the marina buildings and the heavy equipment. Islanders were the beneficiaries of his hobbies, because he and Doug Moreton loved to grade the roads on the upper island, just for fun. And woe to anyone who did not keep his lawn mowed to a reasonable length, for Pete would mow it and the islander would feel beholden.

Another project in which Taggares was involved was the cleaning out of the pond adjacent to the bathtub house. He, Tom Crowley, and Harold Bartram joined forces in this volunteer endeavor. The pond was the old log retaining pond from the Spencer Mill days. The men also built a small dam to keep it from running out into the bay. Molly Crowley brought lunch to the gang one day and is quoted as asking why they weren't out playing golf on Orcas or something instead of this dirty work. Taggares replied that this was lots more fun than chasing a little white ball around. He did build a large yacht with a helicopter pad, so he could come and go easily to manage his eastern Washington businesses when he was out cruising in the Gulf Islands. Unfortunately, just when he was able to work less and enjoy life more, Pete died on February 29, 1999.

If ever anyone looked like the stereotypical desert rat, it was Doug Moreton from Wickenburg, Arizona. He was an accomplished engineer and creator of Skydrol, the flammable-resistant hydraulic fluid used by most aircraft. Willing to discuss any problem with a fellow homeowner and usually dressed in khakis and a battered cap, he would squat down on his heels sucking on a dead cigar and talk. For years he and his family lived above the hangar (73) at the center of the airstrip. Later he bought Lot 1 of the 30 lots reserved by Tom Crowley as part of the Syre-Crowley agreement. It was on Spencer Lake across from SPU, and he and his wife Elinor enjoyed several years in a newly built home there, before both became unable to fly to the island from Arizona any more. Friends say he was quick to offer assistance to anyone and, like

Pete Taggares, often graded roads just for fun. Dr. Shaw recalls that, when SPU was building a short dock on Spencer Lake below the campus (a shore called Sunshine Bay), the dozer tipped over at a 45-degree angle, whereupon Moreton appeared by magic from across the lake to help them right it.

Another magnate who raised eyebrows was Dean T. Mohler (28), who built a three-story home that cascaded down the steep hill at the west corner of the development. The home often vibrated with music and merriment from the recreation room frequented by friends of their children. It was the venue for several New Year's Eve parties. Peter "P.J." Pringle often enlivened the party with his wonderful piano playing and was joined by other Blakely musicians. Dean made his fortune with Dairy Queen franchises in Canada and, having worked hard all his life, prepared to enjoy the fruits of his labor. Within a few years of this burst of preparation for retirement he died suddenly, leaving his wife and children to cope.

One of Blakely's colorful and friendly characters, who passed on in the 1990s, was Martin "Cap" Guchee (129). His lifetime career was in the maritime field as a captain of tug boats that plied the coastal waters from Seattle to Alaska. During World War II he made many trips to supply the Aleutian Islands at a time when the Japanese were threatening the small, remote islands of the chain. After things calmed down there, he was assigned to tow barges of material from San Francisco and Seattle to the Marshall Islands of the South Pacific. His adventures and memoirs are recorded in a small book by Helen Leber, an Anacortes neighbor in Guchees' later years, published as *Northwest Tugboat Captain, the Life and Times of Captain Martin Guchee, 1905-* , a book that might be available in Northwest libraries. When Martin and Helen Guchee built their home on Blakely, they never quite left the sea. The home juts out from the steep slope like the bow of a tug.

Guchee had a slight limp from a boat accident, but the insider joke at Blakely was that he got the limp from walking across the steep hill between his house and that of Dick Campbell to visit or have refreshments.

One of the oldest cabin owners on Blakely, Bill Beebe, was a prankster and close friend of Don and Betty Fitzpatrick. When the

Fitzes built their cabin, they used some non-matching lumber and, being artistic, painted several panels of the house in different colors. Beebe thought this was awful. When the Fitzes arrived at the island one weekend, they found that Beebe had wrapped the entire house in matching colored paper.

Current owners of the Beebe homesite, Ralph and Cindy Zeck, found more Beebe whimsy at the original house. When they tore paneling off the walls, they found that Bill had written entertaining notes on the framing lumber before covering them with the paneling. He noted that Richard Nixon was the president at "this" date. At another site he commented "that scoundrel is still in office" (probably still Nixon). Bill also made a practice of attaching a note to every piece of furniture and equipment he owned, stating its purchase price and date-even to items like a garden hoe. A conscientious flyer Bill announced on Unicom one day that he was crossing the south end of the runway, then returned to the mike moments later to say sheepishly that was not crossing yet because he had revved up his motor and discovered he was still attached to his concrete tiedown

Jacques Meslin (SP-2) was born in Casablanca, Morocco, where his family had lived since the early 20th century. His heavy equipment dealership was nationalized forcibly by the Moroccan government in the 1960s, causing him and his family that included baby Coralee to leave the country without delay. During World War II Jacques was a member of the French underground in Europe, fighting against the German occupiers of France and enduring harrowing adventures.

An early homeowner on the island, Roger Baird (9), brought the ponies of his two daughters, Cheryl (Pflug) and Colleen, on the island in summer. They kept them in the pasture near Horseshoe Lake and carried water to them each day. Riding the endless logging roads and trails of Blakely was a wonderful adventure. A photo of the two girls riding on Blakely was included in article about San Juan Islands life for Travel/Holiday in 1969. Around 1970, while the Bairds were headed for the island, their horse trailer overturned at the Arlington exit from I-5. Cheryl's pony sustained a dislocation of its hind fetlock area (ankle).. The family decided to continue via Orcas to Obstruction Pass and over to Blakely on the small barge Pack-it. It became obvious that the pony was not going to recover by itself, so the Bairds summoned a veterinarian. Borrowing Doug Moreton's generator the vet x-rayed the injured member and, after anesthesizing the pony, put a walking cast on its leg all the way to its body. Cheryl's job was to sit on the pony's neck and poke it in the corner of its eye to check on whether it was waking up from the anesthesia. The pony never had it so good all summer, earning everyone's sympathy and affectionate pats. JoAnn and Denise Burkhart kept two horses at Obstruction Pass and boated over for riding on Orcas. The only things their city horses feared were Scottish Highland cattle and bald eagles overhead.

An imaginative and jolly prankster at Blakely, Jerry Pringle, donned a more serious hat when he went to work. He was a Member of Parliament for Canada, dealing with weighty matters. Chet and Bonnie Henson were Eastern Washington farmers whose vacation hobby was scuba diving all over the world, including diving on old World War II wrecks in the South Pacific. Former resident Galia Haggard (122) fled the Communist Russia regime by walking across Siberia, enduring great hardship to reach freedom in the Alaska and the Lower 48. Wilbur and Vera Patterson (88) both held Ph.D. degrees and taught at the University of Chicago until retirement. The Pattersons claimed to have discovered the cure to the common cold but said, because the cure was so simple, the Food & Drug Administration refused to consider the testing necessary to put the product on the market. Unfortunately, that cure was not divulged to the public. Don and Betty Fitzpatrick Sr.(14) were founders of the huge Fitz Auto Parts business in Seattle and beyond. An earlier resident, Dave Myers (46) was known as the "Lettuce King" from Salinas, California, and married a summer-time waitress from the Blakely Restaurant named Irene Johnson of Bellingham. These are only a few of the memorable homeowners, some alive and some not, of San Juan Aviation Estates.

When completed in February 1984 the Thomas B. Crowley Laboratory housed a laboratory space, offices, residences, and a dining area. The complex was dedicated in May 1984, and Dr. Ross and his wife moved into their living quarters in September 1983. More than 100 dignitaries attended the dedication, including Senator Slade Gorton, as well as several Blakely residents who all were invited to the event. Shaw said that, when he flew, the senator required a plane with two engines and two pilots.

In 1984 a Blakely hydroelectric plant was up and running near the site of the old Thatcher Bay Mill, which also had been operated by hydropower in the same canyon that leads from Spencer Lake to the sea before 1900. The later plant used a turbine with a 9-3/4 Pelton wheel driven through a 12-inch penstock from Spencer with about 3 cu.ft./sec. of water at a nominal head of about 200 feet. Power produced is turned into the OPALCO grid. The whole project was underwritten by home-owner John Leslie (lot D), who did not ask for any reimbursement. Leslie simply hated to see water power go to waste and hired a professional engineering company CH2MHill (the firm of Blakely resident Jim Poirot, (31) to construct the plant. It now is a source of study for science and engineering students at the SPU facility.

The researchers at SPU uncovered interesting insights into Blakely creatures. A Marine Invertebrates class taught by Dr. Ross Shaw concentrated in studies of sea life at Armitage and Thatcher Bay, as well as both lakes. The researchers found that a strand of Sea Pens existed just north of Thatcher Bay, not known in those waters previously. One project was the identification and photographing of the sea life that lives on the submerged rocks of Peavine Pass. Bull kelp is common along the shores. Did you know that one can make pickles out of this kelp?

Researchers learned that six species of bats exist on the island. Two of the species, the long-legged bat and the silver-haired bat, are either rare or endangered and must be left alone. Bats do carry rabies sometimes, although very rarely on the western side of the North Cascades, so beware of contact. SPU professors noted that the Douglas Squirrel, a non-hibernating tree squirrel, is native to Blakely. Beach walkers frequently see river otters, because they have adapted to salt water over time. Local sea otters were decimated decades ago, but lately a few have been seen again in Puget Sound south of Port Townsend. The two kinds are difficult to tell apart, but one difference is that sea otters will roll over on their backs but river otters never do. I remember seeing a sea otter at Seattle Aquarium lying comfortably on its back and cradling its baby.

A young summer student at SPU, Robin Shannon, wrote this lovely poem from the perspective of a silver-haired bat:

Darkness falls as I awake, nighttime is my lifetime,
Upside down is rightside up, confusion means clarity.
Seeing is sensing, bugs lean and scarce,
Hungry, cold, endangered, no place to go.
Humans everywhere seem to suck our blood dry.
We hide, they seek, they come, we die.
I sleep at day, in the night I prey.

The sparse numbers of summer students at SPU's campus include those in accounting, biology, photography, writing, and marine studies. One group catalogued flowers and trees and found that in two areas of sun and sparse soil the island has plants common to eastern Washington's dry climate: death camas (yes, if you eat the bulbs, you die but some other camas is edible), prickly pear cactus, woody sun-flower, larkspur and others. Ten species of flowering plants live entirely under water in the lakes. Birds sighted include cedar waxwings, killdeer, cowbirds, and band-tailed pigeons, as well as the more common ones like the raven, crow, eagle, swallow, and seagull. During a pioneer class program at the bathtub house a tiny, rare blue spruce bird was seen.

The raccoons native to the island for many years adopted SPU's campus personnel, and initially the kitchen staff got rid of fully half their garbage by feeding it to them. The practice got out of hand, however. The Shaws used some fish fertilizer on potted plants around the campus. One morning they found all the pots upset with dirt all over the place. The raccoons had been searching for the fish they smelled. At the settlement a few homeowners fed the critters, too, and they became quite bold and messy, spending their nights on the homeowners' decks. Because people were concerned about possible attacks on small children or pets, the practice of feeding them was discouraged strongly-no matter how cute they were when they looked into one's living room window at night. About 1999 a virus that swept Blakely and other islands decimated the raccoons, but in 2005 a few have been seen once again in the settlement.

The anchored swim raft is the target for swimmers at Horseshoe Lake in the 1980's

Good fishing from a raft on Spencer Lake. Del and Dorothy Ennen of Bellingham.

Children and a few adults steeled themselves to jump off ever higher cliffs at Horseshoe Lake

The rope swing on Horseshoe Lake

Christmas Ship courtesy of J & J Tompkins. Inset: Santa with Anna.

Helen and "Cap" Guchee are not too old for Santa Claus

Blakelyites board the Paraclete at Anacortes for passage to the island.

A crowd of Blakelyites welcome the Christmas ship.

The Big Snow of 1996

The Big Snow of 1996.

The Big Snow of 1996, "Hey! Can't Move!" Krissy Burkhart.

Residents enjoy a music event at Ken Parker's.

Fire destroys the Norberg Home at SBA in 2005.

Chapter X
THE WAY IT WAS AND IS

Gaining knowledge is always important, and in the 1960s to 1970s world leaders often staged Summit Conferences. Thus, when Blakelyites wanted to spend a pleasant summer evening in a scenic location, they staged conferences at Blakely Summit. Participants loaded up potluck food, appetizers, and beer or margaritas to travel the extremely rugged road (then) up to the summit. In one spot a vehicle would lean alarmingly as it ran over a large boulder. Islanders spread picnic cloths and picked out a favorite rock to sit on, fought off the yellowjackets, ate, drank, and talked until the sun went down. It is doubtful that much weighty knowledge or research resulted from these conferences but certainly great fellowship. The terrain at the summit was so rough, though, that during one conference when Bob Sumner tripped and fell, he rolled a great distance down the rocky hill until he could stop. By 2005 the trees have grown so tall that the view is somewhat obscured from the mountain, but peak experiences (the current slang) still occur.

Blakely teens were as creative in their recreational pursuits as their parents, if not more so. Small children gathered sand dollars and dug for clams. They brought them home in pails, demanding that their parents cook up clam chowder. The spreading tree at the south beach was always a favorite haven for overnights by children, although sand fleas bothered some Children painted rocks and sold them at the marina. Others baked decadently delicious brownies or cookies and set up sales stands.

At Horseshoe Lake, always popular for water sports, to this day Blakely youths proceed through another rite of passage by jumping off the diving rocks (ever-higher cliffs at mid-lake) into the very deep water there. For several years a wonderful rope swing was the prime gathering spot for good swimmers. It was engineered under the leadership of the Strausz boys. A solid tree that leaned at a 45-degree angle near the shoreline was the focal point for a stout, large diameter rope with a big knot at its end. One would climb up the steep bank and shove off over the water. At the zenith of the outward swing the person dropped off into the water, feet first. Even a few adults tried the exciting rope swing. Dr. Ross Shaw claimed concern about insurance liability and, since the rope was on the conservation easement managed by SPU, they asked an associate from Camp Casey to take a look. He reported that the branches where the rope swing was located had internal rot and proceeded to cut down the tree, putting an end to the delights of the rope swing. (Understandably the demise of the tree and rope was highly unpopular and the necessity of cutting it questioned.).

Across from the rope swing Zan Strausz and friends once installed a platform about 30 feet high, used by some of the more intrepid older children. They jumped in not dove; Scott Burkhart did dive in one time only and said his head hurt all day. Deeming the platform to be too dangerous even for themselves, and especially since the lumber was deteriorating, the youths dismantled it.

From the beginning of the SJAYE generations of homeowners' children have enjoyed a Huckleberry Finn type of life. Pre-teens then and now had camp-outs (no fires, of course) at Horseshoe Lake's cabin area. Typically they told each other about the ghosts of the cabin, that a dead sheep was buried underneath it, and such tales until no one dared to sleep and went skinny-dipping at midnight, instead. Older teens had Blakely Peak picnics with a rite of passage being the ability to ride a motorcycle up there and back down in pitch darkness. June Bartram, Shelley Burkhart, Janet Reece, and Cindy Carruthers recounted tales of driving the jeep around on the upper island until they were "dustballs," then going into the lake fully dressed to clean up. Rob Lynch said that the only way to get to the upper island in his teens was to tackle the original "Old Steepie" in 4-wheel-drive low range low.

As the center of summer activities for islanders Horseshoe Lake's few amenities were generously provided by volunteers, In 1973, a boat dock was erected to serve those with small boats by a committee headed by Jim Bridge and built by volunteers that included John Conway, Carl Bridge, David Welch, Jim and Joan Fergus, and Lance Douglas. Since the 1970s Don Burkhart and Lance Douglas have been very active in maintaining facilities at the lake. With some help from locals the men hauled in sand to the entry beach several times and, in 1981, Burkhart rebuilt the shore dock atop concrete pillars, after monitoring the lake levels for several seasons. The dock was designed to be submerged by no more than two inches of water at the highest winter water level, thus assuring it would not be too tall to reach at low-level times in late August. Unfortunately, for some unknown reason. Pete Taggares installed a weir that raised the level of the small dam that controls the overflow toward Spencer Lake, and the dock (now 25 years old) is covered with as much as 12 inches of water at times. Plans are afoot to rebuild it.

In 1991 Burkhart and Douglas, with the help of Anne Malmo, David Welch, Jim and Joan Fergus, and perhaps others, also built a replacement swimming raft to be docked out in the water a short distance as a destination for swimmers. The original one had rotted away. Don used his scuba gear to anchor the platform to the bottom. That raft breaks its chain every few years during high winter winds and floats away to anywhere on the lake. The two men regularly rescue it, and Don re-attaches it to the anchor. Later they also built a replacement boat dock with lumber and materials donated by many residents.

Lance Douglas plus a woodworker from Orcas and others voluntarily rebuilt the old homesteader's cabin at Horseshoe into a haven for changing clothes or throwing down a backpack while swimming. The crew searched the forest for naturally bent logs for the unusual railings. Half the money for costs came from community members and half from BC Crowley.

The habit of volunteering and the feeling of ownership in their island is built into the psyche of the islanders, beginning as early as 1962, when several islanders-Floyd Johnson, Les Edminster, Gordon Willie, George Wilson, Del Taylor, their wives and families—restored the old schoolhouse as a permanent museum to depict how school rooms looked in the days of the Spencers, Menzies, and Straub. Edna and Glenn Taylor refinished the old pedal organ. Volunteers installed a metal grillwork door, so visitors could see but not damage the school-house. Today's residents see that required maintenance occurs, so the roof doesn't leak or the small porch fall in.

As the number of residents grew, so did regulations over the years, although great effort was made to keep regulations and traffic signs to a minimum, especially the latter, to retain the country not city atmosphere. In 1970, the board passed resolutions suggesting that children under the age of 12 should not drive motor vehicles, that helmets for riders and spark arrestors and mufflers for motorcycles should be encouraged by parents, and that Blakely air strip should be classified as PRIVATE, restricted to owners and guests (plus service personnel such as charter aircraft and scheduled airlines, of course). As early as 1971, the board began debate about the plethora of small boats at Horseshoe's swimming area and made plans to ask volunteers to build the now-existing dock near the lake's outlet, instead. In the 1990s the boats and canoes were made Commission property for the use of all owners, and others were removed from the lake. Likewise, for many early years SJAYE owners and SBA owner donated funds to underwrite the stocking of the lake with young trout. Tennis players donated funds to maintain the tennis court built in 1979 as a separate, non-profit corporation. In 1986 BIMC accepted title to the tennis court and assumed its maintenance plus the cost of stocking Horseshoe Lake with trout fingerlings, as mentioned in an earlier chapter.

The question of hiring a full-time caretaker first came up in 1977. Until then volunteers came forward to help with some of the tasks. Ward Weiland (113) was hired for some work during 1972 and 1973, and for a few years thereafter there was no caretaker. In 1979, the hired employee backed out at the last minute, and Blakely resident Phyllis Tucker performed some of the caretaker duties during that year. Scott McCulloch agreed to help out part-time. He said only about 10 homeowners spent winters at the island, and it was a bit lonesome then. The Hamilton house was leased to provide a home for him temporarily. Caretakers Jack Dunster (wife Faye) was hired as an official caretaker in 1986 out of 200 applicants. Inevitably, he became dubbed "Dumpster." However, a few years after his acceptance of the job, unforeseen problems caused him to terminate his employment.. Over the last 20 years the duties and responsibilities have changed a little here and there but the essence remains. Michael "Mick" Moore and wife Esther were caretakers serving after Dunster until Mick's resignation in 1991, Ken Parker agreed to serve until 1992, and Jim and Margo Davis were hired in 1993.

At this writing in 2005, Jim Davis is the current Facilities Manager (formerly the job was named caretaker) of BIMC. Both Jim and Margo undertook studies to both attain the designation "Water Level Operator II" and Jim "Water Distribution Manager I." Prior to hiring caretakers or managers the individual board members responsible for water, airport, etc., performed more hands-on duties than today. Basically, the caretaker's duties are to supervise the operation of the water system, operate the post office and UPS receiving station, police the settlement, watch for open doors on owners' homes that might cause damage to the interiors from weather exposure, do fire patrol and truck maintenance, and a host of other duties to make the settlement run smoothly. Quarters were made available for the caretakers. After the Hamilton house was no longer available, former owners Chuck and Jan White rented their south-end Panabode cabin to BIMC as a caretaker dwelling. The home of original owners Dick Alley (116) was acquired by BIMC in the 1980s as a caretaker dwelling. The Moores were the first occupants, then Parker, and now Jim and Margo Davis at this writing.

Originally SJAYE owners brought their garbage to an open dump back in the forest about a quarter mile from Horseshoe Lake. In 1989 long-time members welcomed a new, more sanitary disposal system that resulted in garbage going off-island but fondly remembered MacNaughton Park" as a splendid place to practice target shooting of Canadian rye bottles and Mrs. Butterworth pancake syrup jars. Pete Taggares undertook to reduce the raccoon population at that dump, as well. Hunting is still permitted on the island under certain regulations. When deer population threatens safety of the airport area, their numbers have been reduced by encouraging a few days of bow hunting around SJAYE. Some years ago a few renegade house cats prospered at the dump and became completely feral, but they have long since disappeared.

A neat recycling building dubbed the BIRD opened in 1989 near the tennis courts, not without some homeowner objection. Lance Douglas spearheaded the effort and spent countless hours working on it, even contributing materials. Originally BIMC actually made a small profit on the recycled materials by selling it to Fibres International of Bellevue, although the BIRD was not created for monetary reasons. It was to reduce the volume of materials going into the compactor at the marina, purchased at that same time. Handling of cardboard and paper has also virtually eliminated the outside burning of trash by residents. In recent years it was impossible to cover costs of recycling, because of transportation rates. In 2005 recycled plastics, mixed paper, and cardboard are accepted by San Juan County if BIMC pays the transportation costs. Blakely managers now try to market aluminum cans on a volunteer basis, persuading anyone leaving the island by truck to haul them off and sell them. The operation is marginally a break-even situation, with the help of Blakely volunteers. Certainly the situation is preferable to "MacNaughton Park," although perhaps not as much fun.

In 1989 OPALCO announced that it would bury its power lines on the development property and urged homeowners to agree to a fee covering the cost of burying lines to homes, as well, which was done. The ditches were not completed until 1991, but eliminating aboveground lines greatly improved the appearance of the plat and minimized power outages.

While the ditches were open for burying power lines to individual homes, Don Burkhart suggested it was a good time to bury some television reception cables, too. He had been maintaining the television system on a volunteer basis for some time. The cabling system was very primitive in the beginning with reception confined to only two or three channels, KVOS Bellingham (12), CBUT/CHEK Victoria (2 and 6, and sometimes channel 8 from Canada. In the early 1970s Chet Henson and a group of north end neighbors mounted an antenna on top of a fir tree at the hill called "Little Steepie;" indeed, it is still there. They extended a cable through the woods to the Adams house, branching westward to Weilands (113), Bob Foster's home (135), and along the road, across the north end of the runway to terminate at Henson's (42). Somewhat later Pete Taggares mounted another antenna at the top of the power line cut and ran it down to his lots and to Fegert and Bartram homes. Scott McCulloch said that he did so originally because his son was playing in the Rose Bowl that year, and Pete wanted to see the game.

Ten years later, Dick Ludeman and south end residents installed a good antenna (the one still in use) on the ridge above Horseshoe Lake, ran a cable through the woods to Tompkins south airport home. From there they installed a distribution system that stretched north as far as Parsons' (106) on the east side of the runway and to Douglas' (30) along the west road to close to Henson's original system. This installation was far superior to the earlier ones and forms the basis for the current system, which has joined portions of the original segments. For a few years many residents usually could receive the Seattle channels (4,5,7,9,11,13). After the system was damaged during winter storms of 1989 and 1991, volunteer Don Burkhart with Doug Moreton and Jim Tompkins replaced 900 feet of cable. BIMC then hired a mainland electronic firm to tune up the system, and thereafter virtually all households were able to receive four to seven channels. The system was upgraded somewhat in 2003. Satellite systems and cell phones have all but eliminated some of these earlier challenges, as well.

During the 1980s and 90s OPALCO installed a remarkable power grid for the islands with overhead lines that traverse Blakely from south to north. The grid uses continuous power lines that pass from island to island by underwater cable in a circular manner. If a power outage occurs from a tree falling on a line or whatever, power can be re-routed to flow in the opposite direction, thus isolating the outage point and enabling power service to all other customers without interruption until repairs are made. The underwater cable from Orcas to Blakely was installed back in February 1958 and the Decatur to Blakely cable in 1961, as well as an updated one from Orcas to Blakely again later.

For the first years of the settlement telephone service was achieved through a small dish mounted on the cliff facing Eastsound. Around 1995 Century Telephone installed a fiber-optic system. In May 1989 a post office building was added to the fire house. Other occurrences around that time included the removal of some trees in the buffer zone that had been downed by the elements. A small amount of sales money was received for the removed trees.

The only way marina operators, facilities managers, and homeowners can access Blakely is by airplane, charter or passenger boat, and private boat. Most of the time access is routine, but unusual weather can make it a nightmare. The northeasters that funnel down through the Fraser River Canyon of British Columbia to scream across the San Juan Islands are relatively harmless in summer, but in winter the storms can cause the temperatures to plummet to below freezing and bring snow on rare occasions. The few winter residents view with awe the big waves slamming onto Driftwood Beach, sometimes throwing spray far up on shore to freeze quickly. Advance weather information is quite accurate today, but in times past the weather information was by observation on site.

On Orcas Island Richard Willis was the founder of the volunteer weather station in 1890, a service kept current by his descendants until the present, although today electronic instruments have taken over. The Willis homestead was located toward Point Lawrence, where the family could oversee Sinclair, Lummi, Blakely, Cypress and the mainland. At the end of each month the Willis family (Richard, then Culver, and John) mailed the daily records to the National Weather Service of the Department of Commerce in North Carolina to be computerized and added to the national records. In 1964 Culver received The Thomas Jefferson Award from the Department for 75 years of service. Early entries are brief, just "five foggy days," or "the heaviest rainfall yet for February." The average temperature at the Willis homestead, probably little different for Blakely, was 70 to 85 degrees in summer and annual rainfall of 29 inches. The Willis's coldest recorded winter was in 1950 with -8 degrees and 19.7 inches of snow. The worst northeaster recorded by Willis was in 1924 with one million board feet of timber blown down (no doubt, this was for Orcas) following a seven-inch rainfall.

It was not the first disaster spawned by unusual weather. In the 1980s heavy snows lodging on the roof caused an enclosed boathouse housing four boats to collapse. The worst damage was to Harold Bartram's lovely 40-foot yacht, and the boathouse itself was a total loss.

The winter weather was particularly fractious in 1989 and 1990. The second northeaster windstorm in less than two years came at the beginning of Christmas week, when many islanders were present. I quote a commentary by resident Karl Leaverton from the board minutes of February 2, 1991:

...And we thought the weather was frightful on December 16th when we left the Island following the board meeting!! Unbelievable, three one hundred year storms in two years....Most of the time was spent without water or electricity making heat and water, precious commodities. OPALCO crews worked feverishly to get power restored by 3:00 p.m. on December 27th. ...Hal Moyer was capable of keeping a pipe running that allowed us to pilfer his supply [water]. At 4:00 a.m. December 28th we were awakened by a tree smashing on to the garage! You don't know what a thrill it is to be awakened by the thunderous blow of a mighty hemlock until you've experienced it.... Power had been knocked out at 3:00 a.m....We had been on the island for 48 hours with 12 hours of electricity and 14 members had been on the island for over a week and were only able to relish the electricity for the last twelve hours. ...stories of a Christmas dinner prepared for the 14 inhabitants of the island at the "cook shack" of Peter and Janet Taggares....It was a true pleasure to see members working together...

While the San Juan Islands rarely get any snow and, if any falls, it soon melts, Christmas season of 1996-97 made records. The entire Pacific Northwest was paralyzed by not inches but feet of snow that fell relentlessly for days. Blakely's runway soon was unusable, because it had about three feet of snow on it plus six-foot drifts. The storm began quietly enough late on December 21 with a two-inch snowfall and more came by Christmas. I arrived on the boat *Paraclete* from Anacortes at dusk on Christmas Eve. The ceiling was not much higher than the boat, and snowflakes were etched into the darkness under the welcome lights of the marina.

The only people on the island after Christmas Day were Wally & JoAnn Weller, Jim & Margo Davis, some relatives of Ken Parker, Hal Moyer, Lance Douglas, Judy and Jim Tompkins (Jim left on the 26th), and the four members of Don Burkhart's family. Temperatures were relatively mild, creating huge icicles, one fully six feet long hanging from the eaves. Don's daughters, Logan and Krissy, called it the "Icicle of Dooooooom." With several inches of snow on the ground an infamous northeaster slammed onto Blakely Island, accompanied by even more snow. Here are excerpts from Don's account of the next few days:

> The cabin's full frontal glass, combined with Christmas lights lining both the eaves of the roof and sixteen feet out at the fringe turned the deck into a well lit stage. Set it was, and what a show to behold. Snow "dust" would swirl down off ... the roof in many vortices, head left, pause for a moment suspended in mid-air, reverse direction, and follow endless and random patterns of the whimsical air currents.

For two days the residents played in the snow. But Mother Nature was not through with the Blakelyites. During Sunday night the 28th a new storm dumped 14 inches more snow on the island, which turned to freezing rain and formed a quarter inch crust on the deep accumulation.

> The sheer volume of snow exceeded my experience.... It pressed against us, drifting [before freezing] four to five feet up the walls, windows and doorways. Walking outside anywhere required careful thought and planning. The entire runway basin was a tempestuous sea, frozen in still form, and rendered in snow. There were waves upon endless waves, swirling, creating, breaking, and everything in between, a fascinating wide-area snow sculpture that no camera could capture.

Beautiful it was, but within hours the temperature rose and rain began to fall to become absorbed by the snow to weigh down heavily on trees and structures.. Ken Parker's guests alerted islanders that a hangar roof was collapsing, one bay at a time. Jim Davis, Don Burkhart, Wally Weller, and Lance Douglas rushed into action to save the planes inside before their roofs collapsed, too. The men tried to winch the planes out without success. Finally they commandeered Langworthy's trackhoe, managed to get it started and—in pitch darkness-got to the hangars and pulled Sherwood's and Davis' planes out to safety.

The troubles continued. Moyer and Douglas lost power for two days. Water supplies began to dwindle, and the break was traced to Meslins' home where the shut-off was located under 16 inches of snow. Meslins had left a window open only an inch and a half, but the living room had drifted snow inside. Culverts were frozen up and did not allow snow melt to dissipate, creating floods here and there. Judy Tompkins at her home at the south end of the airport had been stranded for days, because it was almost impossible to walk through the crusted snow. Eventually everything returned to approximately normal in time for the New Year's Eve party at Mohler's home hosted by Terry Pence, who had arrived on the island.

Not weather-related at all, the most recent accident at Blakely occurred in April 2005. . Deborah and Dr. Darrell Davey (113) were doing some work at the island that necessitated hiring a mechanic from Bellingham. While transporting him home, Davey's plane went into the water off the Peapod Rocks for reasons as yet undetermined. The passenger survived, but Davey perished from hypothermia. The Blakely "family" agonized with Deborah and her children and praised Darrell for sharing his medical expertise whenever he was needed on the island.

When Floyd Johnson sold his remaining lots and retired in late 1985, Judy Tompkins, his office manager, obtained her real estate broker's license and has since operated her offices on Blakely as Flying Island Realty. Waterfront lots in 1986 were around $75,000 and non-waterfront about $35,000. Houses varied in price from a fixer-upper at $99,000 to $189,500 for a 3-bedroom home with many amenities In 2005 the prices are at least twice that sum.

Presently the Thomas J. Crowley Laboratory consists of the following buildings: dormitory housing 20 students with two apartments for the resident director and teaching faculty; dining hall; library-classroom building accommodating 24 students and staff; dive shop building with an air compressor for SCUBA equipment, showers, dressing room, and small shop. Outside usually are small boats and a 17-foot whaler for use on the Sound. Summer courses offered included "Natural History of Blakely Island," "Marine Invertebrate Zoology," and other. Researchers combing the wilderness areas of the island found trees up to four feet in diameter that had died a natural death, and noted that deer browsed enthusiastically on young firs while leaving hemlock alone. Also present in the forest are red cedar, western yew, and Garry oak, the latter two being somewhat rare. Under the Crowley easement the land is managed as a working forest so that trees may be removed selectively for its health.

Among the interesting studies by SPU is one that describes the harbor seals that commonly hang out on the rock just off the east end of Peavine Pass. The harbor seal weighs about 250 pounds, has been clocked swimming at 9-15 MPH and can stay under water for as much as 30 minutes. At one time it was blamed for decimating salmon runs; indeed, between 1940 and 1960 a bounty of $3 to $4 per seal was posted by the government. It was found that, although they do swim around river mouths sometimes, they take few salmon and that their diet is mostly slow-swimming fish like hake, flounder, and such. During the fur trading years harbor seals were valued for their coats to make sealskin coats for Germans, Icelanders, and Japanese primarily. Their pelt was worth about $12 and the meat sold for pet food. Today they are protected.

Dr. Ross Shaw presided over the SPU property until he retired in 1996 after 20 years on the island. Taking his place were Leroy Hubbert as campus manager and Bruce Congdon in charge of the educational courses. Then came Rick Ridgeway and, at this writing, Tim Nelson, a former SPU student with a degree in marine botany who had studied at the Blakely campus during university days is the manager.

Today the San Juan Aviation Estates have more than 100 homes, most of which are seasonal retreats, plus some guest houses. Only a half dozen families live there all year, because of the isolation during occasional bad weather. No one person sparks the development now, as was the case during the 1950s to 1980s, the days of the Johnsons. The facilities manager and marina personnel monitor the basic systems all year, and a few retirees spend several winter months Judy Tompkins operates the Flying Island Real Estate office year-round.

Original developer of the San Juan Aviation Estates, Floyd Johnson and his second wife Joan continued to live a peaceful, retired existence at Blakely and in Arizona. After Floyd's death on May 12, 1988, his ashes were brought to Blakely and placed in an unidentified location.

Joan lived in Scotland, the country of her birth, until she died September 28th, 2005.

The island mourned the passing of Floyd Johnson, a visionary who, against considerable odds, managed to forge a development like no other in the islands. Because so much of the wild island has been set aside as a conservancy, the unusual playground that residents enjoy is unlikely to change much in the future.

In her memoirs Shirley Plummer wrote about Blakely Island: "I can look down into the clear water of the lake or at the clean-ness of the hills and trees and Blakely holds me. I can never give you what I had. I wish I could, it was a beautiful life. We didn't have 'things' but we had something better. We had Blakely."

In 2005 we Blakely residents have a plethora of "things," but we, our children and grand-children seldom flaunt them to our fellow islanders, because we have something better, too. We have Blakely.

BIBLIOGRAPHY

Belanger, Herb. "Ideal Office-Residence," *The Seattle Times*, November 15, 1964.

Blakely Island Maintenance Commission minutes, various.

Blakely Quarterly (The). Seattle Pacific University newsletter, many editions.

Clark, Earl. "The Pace is Leisurely in the San Juans," *Chevron USA*. Fall 1971.

Coffelt, Joan Wikman, and Robert J. Coffelt. *Times and Lives of Some Coffelts in America*. Coffelt Publishing Company, 1995.

Connelly, Dolly. "Blakely Island's Revolving House," *The Seattle Times*, June 16, 1963.

_____. "Island Airdromes," *Air West*, June 1964

_____. "Isle of Happy Landings," *The Seattle Times*, September 28, 1958.

_____. "A Pacific Northwest Artist at Work," *The Seattle Times*, May 5, 1963.

Crosby, Bill and Steven R. Lorton. "Paradise Found in the San Juans," *Sunset*, August 1996.

Davies, R.E.G., and I.E. Quastler. *Commuter Airlines of the United States*. Washington and London: Smithsonian Institution Press, 1996.

Gunther, Erna. *Indian Life*. Chicago: University of Chicago Press, 1972.

Harriss, Bayliss. "Blakely Island Dam Breaks Destroys Many Landmarks," *Friday Harbor Journal*, February 4, 1965.

Hodde, Jane Barfoot. "Obstruction Island Lights," personal research paper from the collection *Memories & Potlucks*, Olga, Washington, 1996.

"Islands with Everything." *Seventy-six Magazine*, September 1961.

Jones-Lamb, Karen. Native American Wives of San Juan Settlers. Lopez Island: Bryin Tirion Publishing, 1994.

Keith, Gordon. *Voices from the Islands*. Gordon Keith, 1982.

Leber, Helen. *Northwest Tugboat Captain*, The Life & Times of Captain Martin Guchee 1905- . Helen Leber, 1990.

Lunzer, Jean Hudson. "Families Fly Away—Literally—To San Juan Retreat," *The Seattle Times*, July 3, 1960.

_____. "It's Always Summer at This Island Hideaway," *Seattle Post-Intelligencer*, June 25, 1961.

McDonald, Lucile. "Curiosities on Rugged Blakely Island," *The Seattle Times*," August 13, 1961.

McKenzie, Jackie. "Flying Couples Weekend in the San Juan Islands,"

Gazette-Times. Corvallis, Oregon, August 9, 1958.

Monahan, Bob. "Seattleite Honored for Saving Drowning Child," *The Seattle Times*," January 27, 1965.

Plummer, Shirley. *Blakely and Me*. Lopez WA,. Personal memoirs.

Richardson, David. *Pig War Islands*. Eastsound WA: Orcas Publishing Company, 1971.

Roe, JoAnn. "Elegance on Orcas Island," *The Oregonian. August 3, 1969.*

_____. *Ghost Camps & Boom Towns*. Bellingham WA: Montevista Press, 2004.

_____. "San Juan Islands." *Aero*, November 1970.

_____. "San Juan Islands of Washington," *Travel/Holiday*, July 1977.

_____. "Treats on the Wet Side ..." *Los Angeles Times Travel*, July 22, 1984.

"San Juan Aviation-Yachting Estates," *Opalco Beacon*, May 1

Thomas, Beth. "Personal Paradise for Pilots," *Flying*. August, 1957.

Various promotional materials. San Juan Aviation & Yachting Estates and Floyd Johnson.

Vouri, Mike. *The Pig War*. Friday Harbor WA: Griffin Bay Bookstore, 1999.

Interviews and Sources: Numerous including : Harold and Betty Bartram, BC Crowley, Vern Coffelt, Shirley and Buck Plummer, Judy Sande, Berna Menzies Clark, Jim Davis, Mary Ritchie, Bev Johansen, Roy Franklin Sr., Don Burkhart, Lance Douglas, Martha Mills Galbraith, San Juan County Records, San Juan Historical Museum, Orcas Island Historical Museum, Lopez Island Historical Museum, Karl Leaverton, John Madden Jr., Ross Shaw, John Madden Sr., Jane Hovde, David Syre, Archie Satterfield, Sam Caruthers, June Bartram, Karen Lamb, Cindy Zeck, Senator Cheryl Pflug, Wally Weller, Scott, Denise, and Shelley Burkhart, Gordon and Robin Plume, Jim and Judy Tompkins, Norma and Rick Reed, Cliff Curtiss, Meredith Keyes, Nancy Chapman, Scott McCulloch, and countless others.